My Wheels Gave Me Wings

A Journey Through Fear and Despair ... into Love and Healing

by

Willow Rockwell

My Wheels Gave Me Wings

FIRST SUNBURY PRESS EDITION
Printed in the United States of America
February 2012

Trade Paperback ISBN: 978-1-62006-030-8
Mobipocket format (Kindle) ISBN: 978-1- 62006-021-5
ePub format (Nook) ISBN: 978-1-62006-022-2

Published by:
Sunbury Press
Camp Hill, PA
www.sunburypress.com

Camp Hill, Pennsylvania   USA

To Myles,
the keeper of my heart,
the flame to my flame,
the father of my child,
and the love of my life.
In this realm and the next . . .

"The wound is the place where
the light enters you."

— Rumi

Foreword

Willow has written a splendid book about life – her life and your life. She deftly lays bare the trials and tribulations of human existence. And with a wisdom gleaned from deep soul-searching she takes you through the thicket of egoic suffering out into the light of unconditional love and unity. In this loving light the mind-generated boundary between the masculine and feminine, passion and peace dissolves into ever-present oneness.

In becoming one with "My Wheels Gave Me Wings" the heart quickens and the soul expands. Why does this happen? Because as soon as you start reading you become aware that Willow, more than a champion bike racer, is a champion athlete of the soul. And when she wins, everyone wins.

Leonard Laskow M.D.
Author of "Healing with Love"

Preface

You may not know what mountain biking is, or who I am, but I'm convinced that it doesn't matter. This is a story about love transmuting fear. This is a story about my path to true healing and acceptance. This is a story that we all live, in our own way and in our own time.

Life is a dance, or in my case, life is a ride. Sometimes it's difficult and treacherous, but in the end we all get where we're going. There are many helping hands along our path; we just need to reach out and allow ourselves to receive the guidance and magic that surrounds us.

Mountain biking is an obscure sport. It is becoming more popular in the United States, but Europeans usually dominate. Mountain-bike racing consists of one-and-a-half hours of maximum aerobic effort on a trail over roots, rocks, uphills, downhills, and sometimes, man-made obstacles. Think about the toughest trail you've ever hiked. That is what a World Cup mountain-bike track can look like.

In the last few years of my career, I've risen to the top of the sport. I've won two Bronze Medals at the World Championships (2009 and 2010), and I led the World Cup Series for a brief time before eventually finishing second in 2010. In 2011, I was expected to reach the very top of the podium, but life had other plans. I found out that I was six weeks pregnant the day before the first World Cup of 2011, so I didn't race. Circumstances compelled me to rediscover myself, reclaim my identity, and admit that I had never loved or respected myself or my body. It was truly a time to heal.

This book chronicles my difficult childhood, my path to near self-destruction, and the role our magical universe played in contributing to my ultimate healing. Within these pages, I shed light on the intense pressure and fear I faced throughout my entire career, and my gradual realization that no amount of winning could ever replace loving or being loved.

Writing this book was a cathartic and soul-bearing process that helped me heal my wounds. It is my fervent hope that you, the reader, will also learn to heal whatever pain lies within you. I believe that a wise lover exists within all of us, and I hope my story encourages you to find yours.

I speak my truth from my experience. Others mentioned in this book may have experienced things differently, and they are entitled to their experience. I have a voice, and this is my story.

Whatever our greatest and darkest fears may be, directly behind them shines the light of renewal and courage. The world is now calling us to open our hearts and set our spirits free.

Come ride with me

As the River Flows

In the spring of 2011, I was ready to conquer the world. Mountain-bike racing isn't exactly battle, but some days it comes pretty close. The training, the discipline, the constant mental fatigue, the tears, the sore body, and the need to put your life on pause . . . all add up to a very narrow focus. To be truly great at endurance sports, most people believe that the sport is all you can do, breathe, and think about. At 33 years of age, I'd been competing for over half my life, and the top of the podium was finally right there.

I finished the 2010 season second overall in the World Cup series, second overall in the International Cycling Union (UCI) rankings, and then I added another Bronze Medal from the World Championships to my collection. My results, combined with my golden-girl image, scored me a two-year contract on the TREK (maker of racing bikes and major sponsor of cyclists) World Racing Team. My goal was simply to win. Specifically, I wanted to win the 2011 World Championships and the Olympics in 2012. The plan seemed perfect. My years of struggle, sacrifice, and love/hate emotions about the sport were finally paying off. This was my time—I had done the physical, spiritual, mental, and emotional work it took to clear my soul and ready my mind.

I boarded the plane to South Africa for team camp and the first World Cup. Finally, it was time to race.

Blissfully unaware of what was to come, I put on my racing "blinders" and proceeded to carry out my mission. At this point in my life, it didn't matter that the reason for the mission was unclear and unhealthy. It only mattered that I had one, and that I was damn close to completing it.

The team camp went smoothly enough. I had my own room and could meditate and relax as I pleased. The sun was shining in Cape Town; and life was simple, although a bit boring. One of the most exciting times of the day was when I could have my first sip of wine—a daily highlight, if you will. It was a chance to quiet the voices in my mind and to stop obsessing about the seat height on my bike, my bloated stomach, or the blemishes popping out on my face.

However normal our practices and routines seemed to be, I started to notice changes within my body that foreshadowed the life altering news I was about to receive. My nights were full of intense and vivid dreams, more so than normal. Once I woke up with a start as I saw a red-tailed hawk land right on my bed. The next night I saw my hands turn into an owl's talons. I dreamt of a jar full of coiled serpents on a shelf, and a giant bear just quietly staring at me. At night, I would often wake up from these dreams in the middle of an orgasm. I noticed how primal I felt and thought it must just be the South African air.

I also noticed I was having some unusual thoughts about the pregnant waitresses at our hotel. They looked very cute to me, and I remember thinking, "That looks nice." They were so happy and relaxed. I had never seen pregnant women as attractive before, and this surprised me. I noticed that they had that glow, and their smiles were warm and inviting.

I was living in a dream world, and the race was coming up fast. I needed to refocus. I wanted to be in my best shape to impress my new team, but the more sit-ups I did, the more bloated my belly looked. I was sick to my stomach for a week, and nothing looked remotely appetizing. Confused and clueless, I just went on the "eat-nothing" plan. With the World Cup approaching in less than two weeks, I wanted to look fast and perfect in my skinsuit.

The team left Cape Town for Pietermaritzburg to compete in a South African national race. It was to be held on the same course as the World Cup the weekend after. It was the perfect chance to dial in the course and build confidence for the big day. The course was perfect, with optimal traction, and I was one with my bike. I named my bike River and trusted it to find the perfect route up and down the mountain.

The full moon was a day away, and I was expecting my period as usual. I did notice that I had no fear on the technical sections of the course. Usually before my period, my fear would increase dramatically. I put the thought out of my mind and continued with my practice. Down came the rain.

As the days went by, I was beginning to feel more and more uncomfortable, so I contacted Grace Ramos, one of my psychic healers, to check in with my body and help my cycle begin. A psychic healer is a person who has the ability to perceive information hidden from the normal senses through extrasensory perception. She immediately asked me, "Any chance of pregnancy?" I told her, "I guess, but I really just feel bitchy and bloated, and all I want is to have my period so I can win this race!" She said she would do what she could, and I set my mind on the task at hand.

I lined up to race in the pouring rain. Although this was just a small South African event prior to the World Cup the next weekend, the field was talented. The track would be the same, so it was a good opportunity to test the legs and the equipment. The track was a grease pit, and I knew my eyes and body were about to go through the ringer. I started fast, and led Irina Kalienteva, the two-time World Champion from Russia, for the first two laps. Suddenly I felt like I was going to fall off my bike. I slowed down, assuming it was my lack of food intake in the last week that was causing the dizziness. I fell back to fourth place but regained some energy on Lap 4 to move back into second. I was pleased with my recovery, vowing to eat during the upcoming week.

By the middle of the next week, I still hadn't gotten my period. I contacted Grace again, and she just replied, "Hmm, I must be missing something. Your womb is not hot like most pregnancies; it's warm and heavy." Now I was starting to get irritated. I needed my period or I was going to feel like shit and not win this race. Two days left to practice and get things going with my body, or else this trip was going to be one long waste of time.

I headed out to the track, and although my energy was low, I rode every section perfectly. I knew that fear wasn't a factor, and that was always one of my biggest hurdles. Before I got in the car to go back to the lodge where I was staying, I noticed that I'd been watching a three-year-old boy pedaling his little tricycle in circles, and I was hypnotized by his cuteness. Again, I put the thought that I might be pregnant out of my mind and wondered how much I should (or shouldn't) eat for lunch.

The day before the race, I woke up with a neck that wouldn't turn left or right. I'd been practicing a form of acupressure called Jin Shin Jyutsu, which uses 26 Safety Energy Locks, or energy sites, along energy pathways that feed life into the body. I referred to the Energy Locks guide to see what point to hold, and what emotion or message was attached to my energy blockage. Number 12 on the neck read: "Not my will but Thy will, submission of the personal consciousness to the direction of the universal mind."

Right then, I knew I'd better do a pregnancy test before I hurled myself down the rock gardens and tortured myself up the climbs. I went out to the garage to get my bike and ran into Pauline, the owner of our hotel.

"Hi, beauty!" she exclaimed. "What a lovely day!"

I tried to remain enthusiastic, but I was obviously distracted. Somehow she mentioned that her daughter had a baby but was also a kick-ass runner. Pauline believed women could be both. I told her it was funny that she mentioned that, as I had a suspicion that I was pregnant and was headed down the mountain to find a pregnancy test. She let out a little scream of excitement and gave me the biggest hug. Funny, I didn't feel excited at all.

As I set off on my bike, I was blessed with a profound thought. I told myself that either way, this was going to be a relief. I was either pregnant and didn't have to line up to torture myself, or I wasn't, and I was here to win. Black and white, clear as day. That was the last rational and peaceful thought I was to have for at least a month. If I'd known that, I would have repeated it like a mantra all the way to the race venue.

I stopped at two pharmacies, but they were both closed. That left me with the only option of purchasing a pregnancy test right at the venue. Great. There I was in my TREK World Racing outfit purchasing a pregnancy test. This did not look good. I had nervous sweats and felt dizzier than ever. I bought the most expensive test I could find and handed my cash to the clerk.

I managed to get from the store to the bathroom and locked myself in the handicapped stall. I took a deep breath and peed on the stick. After the longest minute in history, PREGNANT showed up in bright blue letters. I took a deep breath and put my hand on my belly.

"Hi, baby, I want you, I love you. This is going to be hard, this is going to be stressful, but please hang on and bear with me. This is not your fault, and I'm not mad at you. I'm going to have more to deal with than I can even imagine, but I can do it, and I will."

I walked outside in the suddenly very bright light and found a small patch of unoccupied grass to collapse in. I needed to call my fiancé, Myles. I couldn't tell the world until I told him. It was the middle of the night for him, and I knew I'd have to try a few times. On the sixth try, he answered with, "Hi, baby, what's going on?"

I just started crying and told him I was pregnant.

"Wow, oh my god, wow," he whispered.

I didn't know what to say, I didn't know how to be. I couldn't believe I was such a wreck. I'd thought about having kids . . .in the same way I'd thought about what car I'd like to drive in the future. A fleeting thought. Not on my radar, not on my list of "things to do."

Myles was amazing as always. He was excited and proud, but very worried for me. As usual, he could see the bigger picture immediately, and knew that this was what I needed, even though it was going to take me a while to get on the page. He knew that the universe had bigger and better plans for us than our own narrow vision. He knew I was a wreck, and he knew I didn't feel safe. He also knew that all my survival fears were going to be triggered. He knew I was going to fall completely apart, but he also knew that that's exactly what needed to happen. And he just stood strong. He told me he loved "us," and would do anything for us.

He also told me that he'd suspected I was pregnant because he'd found chocolate in the fridge the day I left. I never eat chocolate! He mentioned that I'd been saying

magical things to him on the phone, and I didn't seem to
be scared of anything on the course.

I started tripping up on my own confused feelings.
Where was that slightest bit of excitement that I could hold
on to? Shouldn't the woman know she's pregnant, and
shouldn't she be the happy one while the guy is freaking
out? That goes to show you right there how my divine
feminine was completely shut down, and my divine
masculine was in heightened warrior form.

As a former Downhill World Champion, Myles knew the
racing scene. He knew it was less than nurturing, and full
of "kids," as he called them—that is, people consumed with
racing and winning above all else. The same people who
were going to be thrown off by my news, just as I was. He
told me I could do this, to call him at anytime, and to just
go out there and get it done. He asked if I wanted to race,
and I said, "No way." In retrospect, I'm proud that as non-
maternal as I was feeling, my instincts to protect myself
and my child kicked in immediately.

I took one more pregnancy test just to be sure, then I
set off to tell the world. First, I told the team owner, Martin
Whiteley, who registered the same shock and amazement
that I had. I then told the team members themselves, who
remained quiet, unsure what to say to me.

I didn't pre-ride the course. I was a zombie. I wasn't
going to race. I ran in to some female racers who almost
immediately asked me if I was going to "keep it." I instantly
realized that as a woman, to fear becoming a mother was
the saddest fear of all. It is the essence of being a woman
to bring new life into this world. To love and nurture is the
true power of all women. I knew that what was being
mirrored to me were just the reactions of how these women
would react in my situation, so I didn't take it personally.

Martin asked if I would announce the race the next day
on Freecaster TV. I said yes, as I wanted to keep him
happy. I needed my job. I had a baby on the way and no
plan B. All there ever was, was a plan A, and plan A was
gone. He set off to create a press release, and I walked
away, more frozen by the second.

I called Myles back, and he just started crying. He was
so full of love and amazement and joy. I was deeply

touched and saddened just the same. When would I feel these feelings? Would I ever? I wondered if I was just a coldhearted ice queen incapable of enjoying the truly meaningful things in life.

The owner of our hotel, Pauline, had worked with my team for years. Even though I was a fresh face, she embraced me right away. She is just that kind of lady. We had already engaged in many conversations prior to my news, and now we were ready to navigate the heavy stuff. Pauline talked to me for a long time about life, divine intervention, and going with the flow. I will always be eternally grateful to her for nurturing me during this time.

After a restless night, I woke up the next morning and headed down to the venue to announce the race. I was met with congratulations, but mostly it all sounded like "Congratulations?!" I knew that people did not know how to react, so I tried not to take anything personally. I just smiled and nodded and did my best to look like I was stable.

As I was becoming more numb by the second, I just kept up the pretense. As I sat in the booth announcing the race, I was struck by the intensity of the looks on the women's faces. They looked like they were about to die. They looked like this was all or nothing, a battle of survival, fight or flight. It didn't look fun. As the gun went off, I felt nothing. I wasn't participating in the race, so it didn't matter to me. In fact, the whole venue seemed like a speck of dust on the planet, and if I could just get out of the booth and onto a plane, I would be okay . . . wouldn't I?

I felt a surge of anger that this race felt like nothing now, and I had spent most of my life convinced that racing was everything. I felt cheated and conned. I felt like a sucker. I just wanted to go home. All of a sudden, I was just Willow. Alone, far from home, pregnant, full of uncertainty, and scared of life. All the old fears were coming back in heavy waves. I pushed them farther down, into their hiding place, and kept announcing the race.

I watched the girls crash, I watched them fight, I watched someone win. And then I was done.

***

I had to go to the venue again the next day to watch the
downhill. Finally, when I couldn't take it anymore, I got on
my bike to ride to the hotel. I got about five minutes up the
hill before I just broke down. Tears rolled down my face as
I sat on the side of the road.

I called Myles. I told him I was scared of everything:
losing my job, my identity, my mission; and my usual
escape routes of drinking, traveling, racing, and training. I
always wanted to take care of myself so that the rug would
never be pulled out from under me. All my planning and all
my sacrifices and all my suffering didn't matter. The rug
got pulled out anyway, and I was broken. I didn't even
know why it hurt so bad, but it did. The illusion of my life,
my safety, and my fame and fortune was melting away. I
was raw, I was scared. I felt like I was six years old again.

I was terribly worried about money and always had
been. I had grown up acutely aware of the fact that money
didn't grow on trees. From what I remember, I was more
stressed about the monthly bills than my parents had
been. I had linked money to survival long before I knew
better. It was just one of the many fears that had been
programmed into me.

I couldn't walk into the dining room for team dinner
that night, as the tears just wouldn't stop. I sat in the
kitchen with Pauline and asked her to get Martin for me. I
told him I was sorry that I was in the kitchen, but I was
freaking out about everything, trying to figure out my next
step, my next source of income. He assured me that our
contract protected my salary and my two year deal, and
everything would be fine. That was enough to get me on
the plane the next day.

After two days of travel, I arrived at the Durango,
Colorado airport. I saw Myles and his son waiting for me,
but they didn't see me. I felt an instant surge of panic and
snuck into the ladies' bathroom. I didn't think I could come
out. The tears were welling up again. This was my life. I
had a fiancé with an eight-year-old, and I was pregnant.
Nothing sounded more mundane or boring to me. And
nothing was freaking me out more. I texted Myles from the

bathroom that he might need to come get me out. I was frozen.

He knocked on the door, and I went straight into his arms without looking at him. We walked silently to the car. I didn't say a word the whole way home. I was practically dead. Myles followed me into my room and sat on the bed. He begged me to sit in his lap, and I did. He told me all the things he'd told me on the phone, only this time I really heard them. I believed him when he told me that he would protect me and provide for me and that he needed me and this baby in his life. I believed him and I relaxed. I thought maybe this darkness was finally over. In reality, the darkness had just begun to fall.

As I adjusted to life at home, I did all the "right" things. I found a midwife, I saw my shaman, I got a massage, I went for walks. I bought the food and made the dinners, and tried to see myself as a nurturing female. I felt okay for about two days. I think I felt okay because I was still numb.

One morning I woke up and went straight to my e-mail. There was a message from Martin saying that the sponsors were reviewing their investments and we needed to talk. That right there was the beginning of a large and rapid downward spiral. As soon as one fear gets triggered, the rest aren't far behind. This is how the subconscious works. It's all programming, and it has been going on for so long that it just shifts into survival mode as soon as it smells fear.

******

2

The Early Years

Survival issues are our deepest fears. We all have them; they just manifest in different ways. For you to understand me and the things I want to share, you will need to know a little about my history. I'm not here to paint a portrait of a victim, but rather to reveal a large thread that makes up the fabric of my being. I am here to be honest, raw, and real.

I struggled with how much to include in this chapter. I love my parents, and I feel protective of my childhood because I don't want to insinuate that they didn't do the best they could. They did. They did the best they could with what they knew at the time. And they were always trying to do the right thing. In fact, there was so much emphasis on doing the right thing that the difficult or painful parts of my childhood were glossed over in the hopes that in ignoring them, they would disappear. Unfortunately, that never works. All of us are molded and shaped by our early childhood experiences. How we perceive the world and the conflicts we face later in life correlate directly with this time period in our lives.

I learned from Louise Hay's book *You Can Heal Your Life* that we "choose" our parents prior to arriving on the Earth plane. I believe that 100 percent, as I know that I had lessons to learn from my mother and father, and they had lessons to learn from me. They are not the same people they were when I was a child, and their beliefs and ways of living have changed considerably. I have healed from the wounds of the past, but what I'm about to relate is what happened back then. Without opening up about my past, the rest of my life, my behaviors, and my struggles wouldn't make sense.

***

My mother was only 18 when she found out she was pregnant with me. She didn't tell my dad until she was three months along, and they mutually decided to end the pregnancy. Waiting at the abortion clinic, their name was called to go to the back. My dad looked at my mom and said, "Are you sure you want to do this? We don't have to." They walked out the front door and bought a skateboard instead. They got married on October 31, 1977, in a Halloween-themed bash.

My parents were free spirits at the time and wanted to have a natural childbirth. They didn't have any money, and they'd heard about "The Farm," a community in Summertown, Tennessee, which had some of the most renowned midwives in the country. Best of all, The Farm's services were free. So Mom and Dad packed up their Volkswagen bus and drove south. I was born two weeks early on December 12, 1977, with the umbilical cord wrapped twice around my neck. I was tiny, at five pounds, three ounces, but I was healthy. I had arrived.

In the 70s, hippies were everywhere. My parents weren't necessarily hippies, per se, but they did love to connect to the earth and the cosmos. My dad, in particular, was intently searching for his truth. He was feeling the need for a change, but he wasn't sure exactly what that change was. His mother was a Seventh Day Adventist, and he had one foot in the waters of religion and one at the other end of the cosmic spectrum.

As my dad put it, they were yearning to be closer to God and often used weed as a sacrament. Sometime around 1980, a group of them went to a "Rainbow Gathering" in West Virginia, and were left disheartened by the experience. They expected to find a way to connect with the universal truth, but the "free love" attitude left them feeling dirty and uninspired. They checked that way of living off their list.

My dad, his brothers, and their friends were building a house for his oldest brother in Clearfield, Pennsylvania. One day he and his brother-in-law were working while partaking in some organic magic mushrooms a friend had grown. When they took the mushrooms, it was in an earnest attempt to go beyond this realm. They began contemplating the existence of God. A strong wind blew through, and houses were collapsing in the surrounding areas. They kept circling back around to the idea of "time, storms, and change." Chaos was surrounding the job site, and not long after, the house fell flat.

A bit later, the local newspaper crew wanted to take some pictures and interview them for a story. My dad climbed into the Saab wagon with his brother and brother-in-law to head back to the construction site. Sitting in the passenger seat, he randomly picked up a Bible. He opened it to read these words out loud: "The Lord is slow to anger, and great in power, and will not acquit the wicked: the Lord hath his way in the whirlwind and in the storm, and the clouds are the dust of his feet." They saw this as a sign that the mighty wind was also a kind and loving wind, and they had the time to make a change and start over again. Both feet were now in the waters of God and religion, and the old way of life was left behind. I was around three at the time, and I don't remember any of this.

Very soon after, my parents relocated to North Carolina with the prospect of more work and eating lots of fresh Georgia peaches. A few brothers and sisters moved with them in the hopes of finding the "Promised Land." They joined a Seventh-Day Adventist Church and became devoutly religious. These are the times I remember.

***

I spent most of my childhood in and around Asheville, North Carolina. I don't have many vivid memories until the around the age of six. During this time I found a teenage neighbor in my bed, and I didn't know what to do. Needless to say, from that time on, I felt that I had a deep and fundamental wound on my soul, which manifested itself in the area of sexuality, specifically. In a sad but all-too-common scenario, I kept silent. Little by little I started building walls around myself to protect the little girl inside.

I don't remember the neighbor in much detail. I remember that he was much taller than I was, with blonde hair, but mostly I remember the feeling: large, imposing, and threatening. I was in bed sick for a time, and the neighbor was allowed access to my room. I remember my cousins and I being friendly with him in the months leading up to this incident, so I guess he was welcome in our home. My parents apparently didn't suspect any foul play. I didn't tell them, and I didn't confront the neighbor either. I was ashamed.

During this time in my life, I made two false beliefs my personal truths: (1) My body and this world are unsafe places to be; and (2) I am not worthy of protection and love and must spend the rest of my life working to get it. Of course, when you're a child, you don't consciously make these statements your reality. They just become your reality.

With those beliefs as a foundation, it doesn't take long for the domino effect to begin. I remember looking in the mirror, saying, "I am Willow," and just realizing that it made no sense. I wasn't in my body—someone or something else was. I was a passenger in a life that I had no control over. Compounding my own beliefs about the world, I was also being inundated by the extreme religious doctrines that my parents now adhered to. If you yourself didn't believe your body was a place of sin, the Seventh-Day Adventist church I grew up in was sure to convince you of it!

The first church I remember was nicknamed "spanker church" for all the spankings we would get outside. Everything was really intense, and I wholeheartedly tried to be the best child I could be. I remember lying awake one night around the age of seven, trying to decide what I would do at the "End of Time." The Seventh-Day Adventists taught that during these times there would be pressure to go to church on Sunday instead of Saturday. If you held strong to your belief that Saturday was the Sabbath and refused to go to church on Sunday, you would be killed. If you were killed, when you got to heaven you would have a red ring around the bottom of your robe signifying that you were a martyr. I decided at a very young age that I would rather be killed than do the "wrong" thing.

A few years later I received a creepy letter from a man at church. I remember him being around me far too much for comfort. He accused me of being a whore, and told me I was going to burn in hell. He also stated that God told him we would be betrothed. This letter made me feel sick. I felt like someone had ripped out my insides and raped my soul. Worst of all, I believed everything he said. His words were burned into me like a brand. It turns out this same man thought Satan had possessed him, and tried to kill Satan by a bridge jump. He ended up paralyzed, in a nut house.

In spite of the confusion characterizing my early years, I have some good memories of my childhood. A benefit of my parents' religious beliefs was that nature was our playground. As the oldest of four children, I took my leadership role seriously. I directed many of our games, and my siblings were willing participants. We didn't have a TV, video games, or many toys, so imagination was key. We would build forts in the woods and can overripe zucchini from the garden for the "long winter." I was obsessed with Little House on the Prairie protagonist Laura Ingalls, so I spent most of my time pretending to be her.

I remember watching the Winter Olympics at someone's house when I was about seven years old. I saw a figure skater on TV and was immediately intrigued. I knew instinctively that the Olympics were a big deal, and I wanted to go. I was in love with gymnastics and begged my parents for lessons. They agreed. I had glory on my mind. At the age of 11 or 12, I created an Olympic Training Program for imaginary clients and my brothers and sister. I had them jumping over my Dad's sawhorses for the hurdles and into the sandbox for the long jump. I put a two-by-four on the back patio and coached my little sister into cartwheels on the "balance beam."

My dad was just getting into road biking, and he encouraged us kids to do the same. Greg LeMond was the hero of the U.S. cycling scene at the time, and the Tour de France was the biggest race in the world. By this time, we finally had a TV, so we watched LeMond win the 1989 Tour de France by eight seconds. We were hooked. Racing was in our blood. My dad made up team time trials for our family to compete in, and we all rode like our lives depended on it. I wanted to be as good at biking as I was at everything else.

Our family would spend hours hiking on the Sabbath, and although it was meant to be fun, there was always an underlying current of anxiety throughout all of our activities relating to our religious beliefs. With my traumatic past and the fear of the "Second Coming of Christ," my survival always felt threatened. We were told the Second Coming of Christ would be preceded by dramatic world events and terror on all levels. After the shakedown, Jesus would return from heaven to take the righteous with him. I especially remember a particular Sabbath Day hike when my cousin Meadow and I went scouting for places to hide for the "End of Time." Not exactly a typical playtime activity for little kids.

I spent an extraordinary amount of effort attempting to be perfect. I was an exceptional student and loved learning, but most of all I liked the praise that resulted from a perfect report card. I studied the Suzuki piano method, and I would play "special music" at church. At the time, I didn't have the greatest relationship with my parents. Mostly, I was afraid of being punished and then rejected for not being perfect enough. I knew the story of how I'd almost been aborted, and it made me self-conscious about my impact on my parents' lives. . I knew they'd made huge sacrifices to start a family so young, and I was desperate to prove that they hadn't made a mistake by keeping me. If there's one word I would use to describe myself as a child, it would be serious.

I believed, because the adults around me told me so, that there was a literal heaven and hell. It wasn't enough to be punished for your transgressions on this earth; there was also a punishment waiting in the afterlife. Hell was a place to burn for the sins of the flesh, eating chocolate, wearing skirts above the knee, and wearing nail polish. Anything that even suggested sex was deemed evil. As a teenager, I liked to read fashion magazines. My dad saw me reading *Allure* one day and told me he didn't like the connotation of that word. All of a sudden, being alluring was evil, too.

I knew I was going to hell; everything was already ruined for me. It didn't stop me from trying to be perfect, though. The perfectionism combined with a complete lack

15

of self-esteem and self-confidence was bound to be the sword that would finally bring me down. I wasn't taught to love myself. In fact, anything related to "self" was considered selfish. I was under the impression that others mattered more than I did, and that others' approval and acceptance was worth far more than my own.

My teenage years were uncomfortable for me. I had plenty of friends at the Seventh-Day Adventist Academy I attended, but I was shy, increasingly uncomfortable being in my own body. I despised the Academy. I found it extremely depressing and devoid of any kind of life force. I desperately wanted to be "normal" and go to public school, but my parents were afraid of letting me interact with the real world.

So I sought solace through sports. Somehow, in those moments when I was working out, my body and soul would connect. My body was not the enemy as long as it performed perfectly. I would get up at 5:30 a.m. to run with my dad before attending the Academy. Then at noon, Meadow and I would do the Cindy Crawford workout video rather than eating lunch. At night, it was gymnastics practice followed by a soccer game. I would go home and eat little or no dinner and throw up when I felt I ate too much. We spent a year of our lives eating next to nothing and watching our hair fall out in clumps in the shower. We needed to stay as close to 90 pounds as possible to be at the top of the gymnastics pyramids. Strangely enough, in this extremely self-destructive phase of my life, I never felt more validated. I received awards for all kinds of sports activities, ran the mile and the 5k the fastest in school, and was told how "light" I was as the boys tossed me up and over the pyramids. This to me was love, and damn it, I worked to get it.

***

My parents never taught me about sex, but I already knew too much for my own liking. I wasn't informed about the female reproductive system or the intimate details of growing up to be a woman. I was, however, ordered not to have sex before marriage. If only the church and my

16

parents knew how convinced I was of the evils of sex, they could have spared themselves the energy of scaring me. I was already scared of everything, most of all myself.

I cannot begin to explain the pain of being in a body you don't want to be in. Only those who have been through similar experiences will know what I mean. It is a constant battle, an everyday nightmare. Every pimple hurts you because it is a concrete example that you're not perfect, but you better keep trying. Every extra ounce of fat on your body feels the same way. A cut on your arm is excruciating because you hurt yourself. The blood gushing out and the tears are just the hidden demons you refuse to admit exist. Having a perfect body was the only conceivable way to ever love it.

By the time mountain biking came around, I was 15, and fully aware that success in sports brought me quite a bit of attention. Maybe it was the fact that other people were praising what my body could do that made it a somewhat tolerable place to live in. I rode my mom's mountain bike a few times before entering the women's "first-timers" race at Cataloochee Mountain. I felt amazing on the one-lap circuit and won the race. I felt like God. Everyone was telling me I was a phenom, exclaiming, "Wow, you're only 15?!" I soaked it up—this false love—and savored every drop.

The next weekend there was a race at Camp Carolina. I was stressed out all week about winning. I didn't. I crashed three or four times and came in second. There was no love, there was no praise, there was nothing. I was left with myself, in this body that wasn't mine, in this world that made no sense, and I was crushed. My subconscious mind decided right then and there that racing was how I was going to prove my worth, and that winning was perfection, wasn't it? I might not go to heaven, but I could sure make my time on this planet better than the hell I often felt it was.

Anyway, I continued on my new mission with the wholeheartedness of a warrior. Every race was the most important, every loss my greatest fear. I was learning on my own, crashing my way through technical sections, and beating up the body I had no respect for anyway.

17

I tore through the ranks, and by the end of my first season, I was racing with the expert women and doing well. My family and I went to the National Race in Helen, Georgia. I won the junior women's category, and the director for USA cycling wanted me to come to Nationals so I could qualify for the World Team. I told him I couldn't, as racing on Saturday was against my religion. So he chose me as the coaches' pick, and I was off to the 1994 World Championships in Vail, Colorado. From that very moment, I saw my future. I wanted to be Juli Furtado. I wanted to be on the Volvo-Cannondale team with Missy Giove and Myles Rockwell. They were the top dogs in the international mountain-bike scene, and I idolized them. Damn it, I wanted to be a star!

I won a lot of races, and I lost a lot of races. I crashed and cried and tried to tell myself that scars didn't matter. Winning mattered, and I was doing it.

I wasn't always perfect. I could be rebellious, too. I liked to lock my door and push the furniture up against it so no one could get in. I would do this when I didn't want to go to church campouts, or when I was trying to push the boundaries of what was acceptable.

Around the age of 16, I attempted this technique to convince my parents I needed to go to public school. It was a battle. First, I had to go to another Academy an hour's drive away. I can't remember why I finally got to go to public school, but after a couple months, I was finally freed to be a "normal" teenager.

I had a hard time fitting into public school; I had no idea how to interact. I wasn't allowed to go out on Friday nights, as I needed to be home by sunset to worship the Sabbath. I met my first boyfriend after three days of attending the new high school, and that pretty much solidified my loner status as far as socializing with other girls was concerned.

When I was 17, I remember trying to decide if I should have sex with my boyfriend or not. I drove my old Volvo out to the forest to read the Bible. I was convinced I was making a life-or-death decision. It was agonizing. I was terrified of being caught and punished, in this realm and the next. Somehow, I came to the conclusion that it was worth the risk. I couldn't imagine marrying someone I'd never had sex with. Now that seemed like a bad decision.

Not long after, my dad gave my boyfriend a letter outlining the sins and repercussions of sex before marriage, and my boyfriend balked. It was terribly confusing. First, I'd put my life on the line for my decision, and now my boyfriend was too freaked out by my dad to continue having sex. I'd already had sex, and now I was being rejected. After a few weeks, I convinced my boyfriend to get over it, but more guilt was now piled on my back.

In my second season of racing, I was sponsored by team DEVO (which supported and trained junior mountain-bike racers), owned by Jon Kemp. I once again attended the World Championships, which were held in Kirchzarten, Germany. I was so shy and quiet that the USA bus left me behind at a gas station. I waited patiently outside for about an hour, and they finally returned to get me. I finished dead last in the race due to a broken derailleur (the part of the bike that shifts the gears). I ran most of the race and returned home with a serious case of shin splints.

After I graduated from high school in 1996, I applied for college. I only applied to one, because that was the school my boyfriend was going to. The University of North Carolina at Asheville was happy to have me. I could have been accepted to many. I got a waitressing job at the Laughing Seed café and continued to train.

During my college years, I discovered alcohol. It liberated me, and I felt fun and attractive. I noticed that people wanted to be around me when I drank. I began to distance myself from my boyfriend, and I discovered flirting. It was a rush to be desired, and I grew addicted to the attention. I'd lost the weight I'd gained from my bingeing-and-purging stage in high school (common in girls with body issues), and I started dressing less like a hippie and more like an undergrad. My grades were perfect, and I wanted to look perfect, too. I had a few close girlfriends in college, but my circle was small. Bike racing was still my main focus.

A local cycling-component company called Cane Creek picked me up for sponsorship. I raced through college and won three Collegiate National titles. I remember when I came home with my first collegiate trophy, my boyfriend slammed the door in my face. He was angry that my brother and I had shared a room in the hotel with a male teammate. I remember standing there stunned. It never took much to convince me that I was unworthy of feeling good. The race I didn't win my junior year is the only one I really remember. I spent an hour crying in the car with my mom, who was unable to console me. She did say, though, "I don't think this is just about the race." She was right.

After graduating from college with a psychology degree, I spent my early 20s on the NORBA (the Board of Trustees that represent the sport of mountain-bike racing for USA cycling) race circuit. I got a lot of attention for being the young woman who wore wigs at parties to garner attention and was actually pretty fast. I was not a Seventh-Day Adventist anymore. In fact, I shut every door to spirituality I could find. To me, when someone said spiritual, they meant religious. Religion had done nothing for me but heighten my guilt and fear, and I wanted nothing to do with it.

I racked up quite a few top-ten finishes on the National circuit, and broke up with my high-school boyfriend to date a guy on the circuit. He was fast and I was young, and in my sober moments, life seemed to be going according to plan. I was drinking way too much, especially after the races. I got away with it when I had a good race, but after a bad one, every stuffed emotion from the last 20 years would come out in a mass of despair and suicidal thoughts. After one bad race, I threatened to jump out of the car, and my boyfriend had to slam on the brakes before I did. Then he called my parents. They didn't know what to say. When I got home, I saw a therapist, but she was old, and I was shut down, and it got me nowhere.

At the end of 2002, I had scored a top-ten at a World Cup and a sixth-place finish at the NORBA national finals. RLX Polo Sport (a division of Ralph Lauren) had their eyes on me. I was 23, flashy, fast, and full of potential. I would have done anything to be on that team, but I didn't get the call until the end of December. They wanted me! And for $25,000 a year for two years, plus bonuses and health insurance. That offer was huge to me at the time. I truly remember the joy of that phone call. I vowed to make them proud. I left myself and my needs out of the equation. I was going to make their decision worth it. From that moment on, bike racing was how I would make a living. Now it was most certainly my everything.

My first race with my new team was a disaster. I finished 18th when I was expected to be in the top 5. My bike worked perfectly, and my team was at the top of their game. I had no one to blame but myself. To this day, it is one of the most painful and heartbreaking nights I can remember. I truly wanted to die. There was no escape from the pain inside, and it was getting bigger than I could fathom after every failure.

Two weeks later I was standing on the podium with the top five finishers at Sea Otter, my first national race against the big girls. I was high as a kite. This is when the real up-and-down swing of my emotions began. I felt the pressure of staying on the podium, impressing my team and impressing myself. When you're close to the top, it hurts even worse when you fall.

Later that season, I finished in a top-ten position in the Vancouver, British Columbia (B.C.) World Cup, and I wanted to party my ass off. Wig on, tight top, short skirt. Done. Of course, I drank half my body weight in vodka and managed to get kicked off the "stage" by the bouncer. I didn't want to kill myself that night, but I did manage to cuss the guy out and start crying for no other reason than that I was pissed and drunk, and well, I had a reason to cry. I would use any excuse to let some of the pain and pressure out of my tiny 5'2" body.

The next day, with swollen eyes and an awful hangover, I headed to Whistler, B.C., with my boyfriend and friends. As wrecked as I was, I was excited that I could continue my party streak. It was my favorite activity, and one I was good at. I always got validation for that, too: "Willow you are so fun, you are so crazy, and you can drink so much!"

Whistler turned out to be what the locals call "Disneyland for Grownups." Dining on a patio with some girlfriends sipping sangria I declared, "I could live here." We spent the night on top of the bar, and it felt like life

21

couldn't get better. The next night I went to another party and spent most of the night on top of the bar again. I spotted a guy in the crowd and asked my friend who he was. "You don't know Richie Schley?" No, I didn't.

Back in North Carolina, I began training for the 2003 World Championships in Switzerland. My boyfriend was in Italy training with some teammates, and I was happy he was gone. We were growing farther apart by the second, and I didn't know how to end it. For me, it was always this combination of disbelief that anyone would want me, combined with the idea that I had to marry whomever I slept with, that kept me in relationships far longer than I should have been in them. I preferred to just let them die out, or sabotage them by kissing another guy. It never seemed like a plan, just an escape route.

I finished 16th at the World Championships and was proud of my very successful season. It was time to celebrate. I headed to Vegas for the bike show. I packed my smallest dresses and my highest boots. You can do whatever you want in Vegas, right? I started partying right where I left off. The first night I got about an hour of sleep, and the second night I found myself in a strip club with a huge crew until 5 a.m. You would have thought I worked there. In fact, I'm sure all the girls there had stories similar to mine. With all the people appreciating my body, maybe I could finally respect it, too. If only it worked like that. The more my body got the praise, the smaller my soul got, and the darker the secrets became. It was just one more way to falsely validate myself so I could avoid looking at my inner pain.

I got kicked out of the club for getting onstage again. I felt so high, I wished I could have just stayed in that dimly lit hellhole, pretending that everyone thought I was beautiful. No one knew if I'd won the last race or not. No one cared. It just seemed like they wanted me. And the wounded little girl in me liked that.

The next night I ended up at the Circle Bar in the Hard Rock Café. Rumors had been circling through the bike world about this crazy cross-country girl named Willow. What a time we had at the strip club last night! As I cruised through the bar, I was approached by a man with the bluest eyes I'd ever seen.

"Can I buy you a drink?" he asked.

"Sure," I replied. "Vodka and cranberry."

"I'm Richie. What's your name?"

"Willow," I replied quite casually.

"Oh, you're Willow! I've heard stories about you." He thought I knew who he was because he was Richie Schley, the big-shot free rider, but I didn't. Free riders make their living by jumping their bikes off cliffs, filming extreme mountain-biking movies, and doing photo shoots for magazines. I thought he was cute. With that simple exchange, a new chapter of my life began.

******

3

A Whistler Fairytale

Before I knew what had happened, I was sitting on Richie's lap at the blackjack table, distracting him from the game. I was 24 years old, straight out of North Carolina, and I was high on the city lights. Yes, I was drunk, but I was also in some sort of trance. We were the only people in the room, and I was oblivious to the eyes watching us. We got in the cab to head to his hotel like it was the most normal thing in the world. Our hot-and-heavy make-out session was cut short by the fact that he had two other guys staying in the room with him. So I just stayed in his bed, and somehow I fell asleep. I must have gotten four whole hours of sleep, the most I'd had in days.

I woke up with a jolt as the curtains were being pulled back to reveal the glaring Las Vegas sunshine. Richie jumped up to get in the shower, but not before throwing a bike magazine my way.

"That's me," he bragged. Okay, so I guess he wanted me to know he was famous.

My mind slowly turning, I remembered I'd arranged a ride to Hollywood with some friends. Shit, my phone was dead, and I didn't remember the name of the crappy hotel we were staying in. As we were leaving his room, Richie asked for my number, and we then shared a cab to the convention center. I continued on by myself to look for my hotel. Finally, I recognized it and yelled at the driver to stop. My friends were literally pulling out of the hotel parking lot, and I jumped in the car. They had packed my bags for me. They asked where I'd been, and I just told them I'd had another crazy night.

As I sat in the car on the way to Hollywood, I could not believe the things I'd done in the last few days. I was horrified with myself and vowed to take it easy that night. My whole body was buzzing, and all I could think about was Richie. I felt like I'd known him for years. I could faintly remember that I had a life in North Carolina, and a

24

boyfriend somewhere, but that life and that boyfriend didn't seem to belong to me. I was done with both of them, and it had only taken three days.

Throughout my life I'd developed a defense mechanism that worked like this: When the shit hit the fan, I'd just pretend it wasn't happening to me. I'd have another drink, act a little crazier, and somehow assume it would all work out. Of course this wasn't going to work forever, but it was working now . . . and now was all that mattered.

When we got to the hotel in Hollywood, I charged my phone up right away. A dozen messages from my boyfriend and one from Richie. I called Richie. We were already planning on how to meet again, how I was going to break up with my boyfriend, and how the hell I was going to deal with my family in North Carolina. I knew they weren't going to like my latest life-changing drama. My home life looked good from the outside, so no one knew I had wanted out of the relationship for a while. It didn't matter what I wanted; it mattered what they wanted. I was used to having my life, body, and mind controlled through guilt and manipulation; I would have to fight once again. I was setting myself up for a massive amount of chaos at home. But I didn't care.

The night started out somewhat mellow, and I told my friend that I'd met someone and wanted out of my relationship. As she was already married, the news was upsetting to her. I could understand that, but I was convinced that if she felt like I did, she would surely understand me. A few drinks in and we headed to the club where we had the local VIP hookup. That's about all it took for everything to get out of control. Again.

Photographers were there, and flashes were going off constantly. Of course I loved that, and worked every angle I could. Before I knew it, we were back at the hotel, and I was looking at a pile of cocaine on a mirror that a local model had brought with her.

"Try it," she told me. "You'll love it, and you'll love yourself."

To hell with it, I thought. I was already in so much shit, I might as well. I put the dollar bill up my nose like a pro, and snorted like my life depended on it. She was right—it felt good.

"Look in the mirror!" she exclaimed. "Don't you feel like God?!" I looked in the mirror, hoping to like what I saw, but what I saw was a mess. A complete and total disaster. A girl out of control, on the ragged edge, and no idea how to get off the train. So I just kept doing lines. That turned into two days, a bathroom full of blood pouring from my nose, a panic attack, smoking weed to try to come down, drinking to ease the pain of it all, and a sweat-soaked night of torture before catching the plane home. This is how I ended a relationship and started a new one.

I talked to my boyfriend on the way home and told him what I'd done. Of course, I left out the part about Richie. He was angry, but also worried about me. He knew how out of control I could be. I collapsed on the bed at home and slept like I hadn't in years.

Richie was calling me, and I was obsessed with seeing him again. I had built a fantasy life with him before I even had the courage to end my current relationship. But I did it, and it was messy. I was full of guilt. I knew I shouldn't have been kissing, calling, and dreaming about Richie, but it was just what happened. It was my reality. It was the chaos I always created to get out of a situation that I felt trapped in.

My family threw a good-bye party for my boyfriend, and many of them sided with him. I cannot tell you how awful that party was. Who comes up with an idea like that, anyway? I was the slut and he was the good guy. But I was used to the judgment and criticism, so I stuffed my feelings of guilt and shame where I always hid them, and went about changing my life. I pretended that I was going to visit a friend and packed my bags again. I was going to visit a friend, that was true. But I had to take a trip to Whistler, B.C., first.

It was clear that this wasn't going to be an easy and smooth start to a relationship. The thing between Richie and me was based on lust and drinking and acting on every impulse that ran through my veins. I was almost 25, yet I had no idea who I was or how to be. I couldn't conceive that any man could truly want anything from me other than sex. I didn't respect myself, and I didn't expect anyone else to, either. From this fragile and dangerous combination came my launching point into a relationship that would challenge every aspect of my being.

Richie and I were together from that moment on. We spent time in California and Whistler, even visiting North Carolina so I could introduce him to my skeptical family. My mom didn't like him because she'd read an interview about him that said he liked women who were 36-24-36, shaven not furred. I guess I could see how a mother would worry about that.No one wanted me to move to Whistler, but of course I did it anyway. Richie and I wanted to be together. I remember when my family came to visit early in the spring of 2004, my dad said to me, "How long do you think this fairytale is going to last?"

The comment stung, but I brushed it off. He didn't understand. Everything about Richie and me was about passion and chemistry. The sex, the fights, the making up, the crying. It was one of those relationships that people warn you about, but when you're in it, you're in complete denial about what's going on.

Like everything in my life, though, I don't look back and regret it. I loved Richie, and being with him allowed tremendous expansion in my being. It was a relationship full of lessons and opportunities, and I grew more from it than I ever had in my life up to that point.

******

4

A Glimpse of My Soul

As the 2004 race season began, I felt like I was in great shape. Physically, anyway. Despite the drinking and the life turmoil, I'd managed to get a solid spring training in with Richie and my friends in California. At my first National race, I was back on the podium. But very soon after, I began a long descent into darkness.

My ex was still racing, and livid with me for moving on so quickly. He was demanding money I didn't have for the things we'd bought together, and my family was unsupportive of my life decisions. Things were tough all around, and my lack of any type of support system was finally getting to me. I couldn't just run away this time. I'd already done that. Now I had to stick out my decision to prove to everyone I was right. I told my mom that Richie was the man I was going to marry.

With the weight of the world on my back, my body felt depleted and exhausted and the race results were just as ugly: 18th, 20th, DNF (did not finish), in the next three races. Of course, this spun me into a depression. When I sucked at racing, I felt worthless. Plain and simple. I came back to Whistler heavy and full of tears. It was rainy and gray there, and that didn't help at all. I was eating too much and trying to force myself to ride for hours in the rain. Everything got darker. I got heavier, and my tears kept falling.

I came home one afternoon from a wet and shitty ride to find a pretty Australian woman named Jacalyne giving Richie a massage. I glanced at her, but then ignored them both. She told me later that when she first saw me, I was screaming "Help!" on the inside.

A few days later, I asked Richie for Jacalyne's number. I needed a massage; I needed something that felt good. She set up her table in our room downstairs and shut the door. She put her hands on my back and said, "Willow, take a deep breath, and release all of this guilt." I was shocked

.I'd never thought about my emotions; I refused to pay attention to them. I simply did not express my emotions, and as a result, my soul was buried. I was only my tortured body and obsessive mind. How could she tell? How could I not have a clue about this myself?

Throughout the massage, Jacalyne kept asking me to breathe, and release certain emotions. With every exhalation, I felt lighter. When we were done with the treatment, she pulled out her notebook and started to draw a graph. The graph went way up and way down. She pointed out that some people have lives that go up and down like this. Some people have lives that are a bit more stable. She told me I was a person with a very up-and-down life. The good news was that I was down as I could be, but I could also be that high. And I could be that high without drugs and alcohol or endless attention. My soul could fly if I would nurture it.

I was ecstatic. No one had ever talked to me like this before. It was like she had tuned me in the station that had been on static for 25 years. It felt right, and I had hope. I knew how depressed I'd been, and now I had something to look forward to—coming back up from the depths of despair. She told me that I was over-trained—the way my legs looked was a clue. She said to put the bike away and focus on how I felt inside for the next few days. She told me not to ride until I wanted to. In fact, when I wanted to, to wait one more day. She gave me an affirmation to practice inhaling light and love while exhaling guilt, fear, and shame: "I choose and give permission to align my soul, sacred heart, mind, and will with love and light." I told her I would take her advice, and I scheduled an appointment for the next week. My soul was awake now, just enough to know it wanted more.

I practiced the mantra. I avoided my bike, and I stopped overeating, I began to feel and look light again. A week went by and Jacalyne was at my door again. We did more breathing work, and then she began to talk to me about entities. She told me that often times when we are dark, we attract dark. Over the years I've learned that when we are not "in" our bodies, all sorts of things come in and disguise themselves as "us": dis-eases, entities or spirits, chronic depression and obsessive thoughts, fear, and so on.

All of the above applied to me. Of course, this scared me. Growing up, all I knew about darkness was the devil. I knew nothing about energies or energy fields or auras. Jacalyne asked if she had permission to remove the entity attached to my being. I said yes.

She was working above my head, and I felt relaxed and happy. All of a sudden I saw this face above me, screaming at me and looking furious. It was me, it was my face, but an ugly and evil version. I breathed deep, and the vision passed. My body felt full of energy and even lighter. I told Jacalyne what I'd seen, and she said she'd seen it, too. The self-destructive part of me had left my body for the time being. The holes in my soul were still there. It was up to me to do the work to fill them with light, or dark would attract dark yet again.

I thanked her and promised to see her again after my trip. I was headed on the road for the next month of races. I was excited. I hadn't been physically training, but a weight the size of my body had been lifted off my shoulders. I couldn't wait to ride.

At the first race in West Virginia, I was in second place until the mud became too much for my tires. I finished sixth, but I knew it was my tires and not my legs. I couldn't wait for the next weekend in Vermont. My massage therapist Debbie gave me the book Conversations with God by Neale Donald Walsch, which dissolved the belief that there was an actual heaven and hell. You cannot believe how this knowledge liberated me. Another ton of weight lifted off my back.

I spent the week in Vermont planting energy around the course in strategic spots. I planned on collecting it as I passed. I talked to the earth and the creatures that lived under it. I asked them to push my wheels as I pedaled. I talked to the trees, I expressed gratitude to the sky. I thanked myself for going through what I had in the last few weeks to make this newfound freedom and energy available to me. I did intervals on Wednesday, and I felt amazing. I knew I was going to win. I told myself that I'd come to this earth to win this race.

Lined up at the start, I told myself to go for it from the gun. This was mine. I knew where the energy was—I was light, and the earth was rooting for me. I hit the start loop first, and by the end of it, I was 30 seconds ahead. I looked back once, and then I never looked back again. I felt magical. I was floating. This had nothing to do with my legs. I didn't even have legs. I was on a soul ride, and I could feel the difference. Nothing could slow me down. It wasn't the fact that I was winning that was so amazing—it was how I felt. I had never felt so good. I had never felt so connected to my body, and so connected to the sky and earth. I had never felt so relaxed. On my last lap, I heard a spectator yell, "Look at it happen!" If he only knew.

I won by three minutes. My parents suddenly had a turnaround in their support of my life. They called me and told me they were booking tickets to come to my next competition. I was hurt that they'd abandoned me when I was struggling and were now back to bask in my glory. But I was used to being praised for what they deemed good behavior, so I tried not to think about it too much. I had my next race to focus on, and I was in exceptional form.

The next weekend I headed to the World Cup in Mt. St. Anne, Quebec. My legs were amazing yet again, and I finished third behind the legendary Gunn-Rita Dahle and Marie-Helen Premont. I finished miles ahead of the three American women who were vying for the 2004 Olympic spot that year. When I saw my flag raised from the podium and popped the bottle of champagne, I told myself, "This is where I belong. The World Cup podium is where it's at." Alison Sydor from Canada finished fourth, and she told me to expect great things to come. I was high, and I was happy.

When I got back to Whistler, I shared all my exciting news with Jacalyne. She told me I was blessed with a gift of grace. I now knew how I could feel. I had tasted the magic. For me, nothing else was worth feeling. It was my new drug.

During one session, she asked me what had happened when I was younger.. I told her my story and let her know that I never had a safe place to talk about it. She asked me to embrace my little girl and tell her she was safe. I was here now; I would take care of her. Besides talking to Meadow, a few close friends and Richie, this was the first time I'd ever acknowledged the pain of what had happened with the teenage neighbor, and it would still be years still before I truly resolved it. But it was a beginning.

******

5

The Learning Years

As 2004 came to a close, Richie and I headed to the Interbike trade show in Las Vegas. As we landed, he announced, "Welcome back, baby. I feel like I've been on the New York-New York roller coaster for about a year." I couldn't have agreed more.

Of course, the lights and the booze and the "sin" seeped into my being once again, and I was carried away by the madness. For all the things about myself I tried to control, there was a part of me that desperately needed out of the box. That part of me always ended up in a self-destructive mess.

At the premiere of the mountain-bike movie Richie starred in, many people asked if I was on coke. I wasn't, but that's just how high I was. As low as I could get, I could also get that high, remember? It excited me that people were paying so much attention to me, and I just got more intense.

I snuck into the shadow boxes where the dancers were, and managed to sneak back out before getting caught. I managed an impromptu photo shoot on the sand with a friend, and of course, drank more vodka than anyone should. A few nights later I locked myself in the bathroom, turned on the water in the tub, and threatened to kill myself. With a razor, I guess. Richie called the security guard, and hearing him at the door was enough for me to realize that yet again, all I wanted was love. I didn't really want to die . . . I just didn't want to live this way.

Jacalyne was there for me, as usual, but I didn't let her know how awful things had actually been for me. I was too embarrassed to ask for real help. Some things had definitely not changed. I was aware that I at least had a soul, and I was aware that I was in pain. That, for me, was the first step. It's hard to look at yourself in the mirror and say, "I have a lot of problems and I'm in a lot of pain."

I remember one party night in particular. I was in Whistler, and Richie was asked to judge a wet T-shirt contest at a club. As I was watching the contest, I felt a huge blackness descend upon me. I felt rage, hatred, and jealousy flowing through me like a powerful drug. I ran out of the club, hailed a taxi to our house, and started packing my bags. Where I was going, I had no idea. I just needed out. I filled up the bathtub again, thinking this time I would really kill myself. Richie came home, and I couldn't even explain what was going on. I had no idea. I was overwhelmed by such profound despair. He turned off the water and gave me a hug. That helped, as always.

One drunk episode would roll into the next, and my drama would never ceased to amaze me. It was like I went on auto-pilot and the demons would just take over. Richie was always worried about me when I would get this way, and I think that validated my actions. I realized that he was always kind, caring, and worried in those situations; and all I ever wanted was to feel safe and protected. The dysfunction of our relationship would continue, with me trying to be perfect to live up to his standards, me realizing that was impossible, and then me completely breaking down.

What I remember most about 2005 is the return to very dysfunctional eating. I was convinced that if I were skinny enough, pretty enough, and debt-free enough, Richie would want to marry me. I was obsessed with him proposing because I thought that would give me the security I so desperately needed. We spent another spring training in Laguna Beach, California. In my fragile state, there was no worse place for me to be. The fancy cars, clothes, tans, fake breasts, and money were all such triggers for me. I felt small, unimportant, and unable to measure up. Richie liked the good life, and I was convinced if I didn't do something to make myself better, he would leave me. So I did the only thing I could do for free: I starved myself. I became hooked on diuretics and laxatives and ate as little as possible. But I would still get out and train.

Sadly enough, I got the validation I was looking for. I was kicking butt at the first races on my new team, Subaru/Gary Fisher Bicycles. I felt like this was where I belonged, and I felt like my weight loss was a key factor in my success. No one ever worried about me. Because the way I was built, I didn't usually look too skinny. I could always get away with torturing myself without anyone intervening.

When I got back from the first races, Richie noticed I was skinnier, and I liked it. I also managed to get rid of all the debt on my credit cards. I wanted to impress Richie with my frugalness. For years I had been trying to live the life of a glamorous athlete on a very small salary. Image was more important to me than financial security. My spending habits made Richie nervous. They made me nervous, too. My shopping sprees could be as out of control as my drinking binges. They would release the pressure, and then bring on the guilt and anxiety. Of course, the whole scenario would have to repeat itself. I was stuck in a predictable yet uncontrollable pattern.

My results in 2005 were good. I didn't win because I kept running out of energy on the last lap, but I did get a lot of second places. I was back on the podium at the World Cup in Mt. St. Anne, but I was miserable. You don't go from winning to getting second and feel good about it. It sucks.

My short-track races were awful, as I had absolutely no glycogen, the body's energy stores, the second day. Most of the races I would finish way down in the pack despite finishing second or third the day before. Of course, no one mentioned I should eat, and it was the last thing I wanted to do.

At the World Championships that year, I finished somewhere in the 20s and decided to party off my disappointment. Richie and I got in a huge fight at one point that night, and he accused me of starving myself. I liked the attention. I'd been working all year to have him notice.

There is one moment of awareness I will never forget. I was skinny, I was debt free, and I was in the middle of another fight with Richie. I shut the door to the bathroom and looked at my naked body in the mirror. I said to myself, "Willow, you have never been so skinny and so

35

miserable." In that moment, a part of me finally realized that being skinny wasn't really going to fix my life.

***

Another winter in Whistler and the rain just kept falling. I picked up a pot habit and would sneak little puffs all day. That lasted for about a month until one day I was sitting on the couch and I thought to myself, "I don't need to train. I've been training all my life. I'm good without practice." I realized that this is how potheads end up on the couch their whole lives. It freaked me out. So I quit smoking. I had to go back to dealing with my destructive thoughts without any safety net.

In the spring of 2006, my relationship with Richie was hitting the skids. Resentments were building up on both sides, and my self-confidence was at an all-time low. I'd stopped taking the diet pills because they'd destroyed my digestive system, but I was still hell-bent on controlling everything I put in my mouth. I was scared of food just like I was scared of money, my emotions, my needs and my body. My body was just something else that could betray me, and if there was anything I could control about it, I was going to do so.

The rest of the year was filled with crashes—both literal and figurative. Looking back, it makes perfect sense. My head just wasn't in the game. My focus was on my faltering relationship with Richie and how on earth I could save it. The answer I came up with was to get breast implants. I was convinced I would be more desirable and would also stop comparing myself to all the girls I thought were hotter. As the race results got worse, I just kept focusing on the newly improved body I was about to get. Maybe I would finally like myself. Maybe I would finally feel worthy of appreciation and love. It was worth a shot.

I didn't have any money for the surgery, so I just put it on my home equity line of credit. I told myself that an investment in myself was a worthy cause. I traveled to Laguna Beach in November and went forward with my plan. I remember the surgeon asking if I really wanted to go through with it. She told me I had nice breasts, and the size I wanted to go to wasn't going to be that much different. I didn't care. I'd made up my mind, and I didn't want to think of other options.

Richie told me I didn't need to, either, but I was stubborn. I'd been obsessing about it for years, and the only way I wasn't going to wonder was to just do it. I don't regret it. I learned a lot about myself and my motivations.

I don't think there's anything wrong with cosmetic surgery, but just like racing, you can do it for the wrong reasons. Every decision or driving force behind my life at that point was from a feeling of worthlessness or lack of love. When a decision is made from that starting point, it will always backfire at some time in the future. I did, however, discover a book that began to change my relationship with my body. The title was Your Body Believes Every Word You Say, by Barbara Hoberman Levine. I sucked up the information and used my new tools to rapidly recover from my surgery. My doctor was very impressed when she saw me a few days later. I had hope. Maybe I could control my body by loving it. Maybe.

Contrary to my new body making my relationship better, things just got worse. On my birthday in December of 2006, Richie and I had an epic blowout. I remember locking myself in my huge walk-in closet and lying on the floor. I looked around at all my clothes and decided it wouldn't be that hard to pack up my things and leave. So I started packing. But something switched in me that night. I honestly think I realized that if my new boobs didn't do the trick, nothing would.

Two days later I tore my ACL in a skiing accident. As I rode down the gondola by myself, I visualized my knee already healing. I used the same visualization I had a few weeks before to see my body working for me, not against me. I didn't heal my knee in the gondola ride, but that sense of empowerment kept me strong as I limped around packing . . . and trying to hide my chest from the world. For all the attention I thought I wanted as a result of getting new breasts, I found that nothing made me feel more vulnerable and insecure than the judgment my decision brought with it. In some ways, I feel that my boob job helped me clear a huge hurdle in my life. The concern with what others thought of me and how I could please them was much more destructive than I'd previously thought.

I had nowhere to go but back to North Carolina, the capital of gossip and judgment. My head hanging low, my shoulders hunched over, I tried to move on with my life. In the unusual way life works, the hardest times turn out to be the greatest blessings. I'd never let anyone know I was having a difficult time in the last few years. I had to stand by my decision to move to Whistler, and I would not admit any pain. It helped to cry, and also to see my long-lost girlfriends. And my ACL injury actually steered me to all sorts of new and exciting discoveries.

An acupuncturist told me about a woman who did Reiki and other types of energy healing. We worked on my knee, and I felt it unraveling and smoothing out. We also worked on me. This woman noticed that I was wearing a small owl necklace and told me that it must be one of my animal totems. I didn't know what she was talking about, but I vowed to find out. I left her office feeling lighter and more encouraged than I had in years. I looked up the owl animal totem, and I found out that it was a symbol of "magic, omens, and wisdom." Apparently, people with this totem were not easily deceived and should trust their intuition. I ate up the knowledge and begun to see signs of the owl everywhere.

I also found a kindred spirit in my orthopedic surgeon, Dr. Steadman. I told him I'd been reading books having to do with the Law of Attraction, and was convinced I was healing my knee on my own. The MRI confirmed my feelings. My ACL was hanging on by a thread, and two weeks earlier it had not been. Dr. Steadman told me that he could perform surgery, but it was up to me. He thought whatever I was doing was working. I decided against surgery and continued on my healing path. I left his office happy and full of hope. I couldn't wait to see how I could heal myself, and I couldn't wait to finally ride my bike. I missed it.

When I look back on the spring and summer of 2007, I'm filled with a sense of awe when I think about the amount of healing that took place during that time. I was still drinking, of course, but with girlfriends and for fun—not for therapy. My whole focus was on healing my knee, my soul, and getting back on my bike. I had no other distractions. Of course, my credit-card bills were huge again, but somehow I let that one slide. My healing was worth it. For once in my life I felt like I was worth whatever it cost to be really happy. Not superficially happy, but really happy.

One day I was riding the training bike watching a Madonna DVD. She mentioned how Kabbalah had helped her see that her challenging relationship with her husband made her a better person. I was intrigued. I bought the Kabbalah book on relationships, and it made me miss Richie. For all our troubles, we did love each other. We were just two wounded kids who didn't know how to heal our pain.

I got into Kabbalah that summer. Too much, in fact. I ended up buying all kinds of things and giving the organization 10 percent of my earnings. Just like tithing in church. It started out innocent enough, but all those things end up putting you right back in a box. A box of right and wrong and what you need to do to ascend. "They" convince you that you're lost without them. I was wearing the red string (a Kabbalah symbol that's supposed to ward off misfortune), and looking at problems as opportunities. I did get that from it. I just wanted faith and something to hold onto.

My knee healed perfectly, and my time on the bike was precious. The last few weeks in February I went to Solvang, California, for a bike camp with my coach. Distracted by the knowledge that Richie was in California at the time, I crashed on the first ride there. Afterward, I took a bath to try to recover. To my surprise, the wood grain of the bathroom door started to look like two owls staring right at me. I burst into tears and couldn't stop crying. I could have filled the bathtub with all my salty tears. I called my cousin Meadow from the tub and sent her a photo from my phone. She was as amazed as I was. If an owl totem was there for me, she was happy. At least it was something.

I felt great on the next rides, and inspired by my mission. The tears were a great catharsis. Richie came to visit a few days later. I met him with resistance at first, but we still loved each other. Maybe the break had done us good. Maybe we would be okay this time. And we were. The spring and summer were great. My racing was great, and Switzerland was my first European World Cup podium. At that point, I knew I'd made it. I was at the top, and I'd only trained for two months before racing began. I knew if I trained harder and longer, I would win next year. The Olympics were coming up, and everyone had their eyes on me. I'd made a huge jump in my performance, and no one had a reason to doubt me—including me.

I over-trained before the World Championships that year and finished a distant 15th. The fall dwindled down, the racing was over, and Richie and I began to have problems again. I was mad that he hadn't proposed like he said he would when we got back together. I was madder still when he told me that he didn't know if he wanted any of those things.

***

We went to a Madonna concert in Vancouver that fall, and my faith in Kabbalah was wiped out with a single realization. The two M's she had on either side of her stage were worth a million each. I realized that she was selling me Kabbalah just like she was selling me her records. I didn't even enjoy the show. In fact, I hated it. I was pissed that I'd been scammed. I went home and packed up my Kabbalah books and sent them back.

I decided to ignore my coaches' advice and go for "death rides" whenever possible. I went out for plenty of four-hour crushing rides with my dad, brothers, and friends. The harder the better. I was ready for World Cups by the middle of February. But energetically, I was dark and heavy. I was in North Carolina, Jacalyne was in Whistler, Kabbalah was ancient history, and my relationship was a nightmare. My body was putting on weight regardless of how hard and long I trained.

I showed up to the first World Cup in Belgium overweight, over-trained, and already over the season. The gun went off, and all of a sudden it was like I literally hit a

brick wall. I went backwards faster than you could
imagine. I finished somewhere in the 50s, unable to believe
what had just happened to me. And it kept happening.
Over and over I was at the back of the pack. I got more
depressed by the moment. I didn't want to kill myself; I was
just trying to understand. There must be a reason, I kept
telling myself.

After a DNF at a World Cup in Spain, I wrote a poem
that was inspired by the bellman in my hotel. I'd told him
my favorite Spanish bike racer was Pedro Delgado. He said,
"Oooh, they always said he was like thunder. When he was
there he was 'WOW,' and when he was not, he was 'muy
mal.'" I laughed and told him I was the same way.

> If Delgado is thunder, then I am rain
> Struggling, suffering, dealing with pain
> It doesn't matter in the end
> Glory fades and beauty dies
> All that's left is what's inside
> And how you deal with ups and downs
> Can you smile when you'd rather frown?
> This is all but a test
> Just wait
> I am not finished yet
> I have surely hit the bottom
> but I am swimming toward the autumn
> It will soon be funny when I look back and think,
> "Man, those three weeks sure did stink!"
> But look how it broke me
> then molded, sculpted, and polished a new me,
> as infinite as the sea
> I am thankful for the pain
> because after the thunder and the rain,
> I can see it's all a game
> This game has been my life of work
> Sometimes I have gone berserk
> Nothing is worth that kind of torture
> so on with the show 'cause I'm a soul searcher

***

In a final attempt to salvage my body and spirit, Jacalyne came to Italy to help me qualify for the Olympic team. It was the World Championships, and if I placed in the top three, I would automatically qualify. With my results from last year, it was totally possible. With my results from this year, it would be a miracle. She worked on my body; we worked on my soul.

I was heavy and depressed, and we cleared most of it out. She believed I was ready to win. I started to believe her. She told me to ride the race for all the people who struggled like I did. Take them all to the finish line. I did feel magical. I had an amazing experience that week that I will never forget. As Jacalyne was working on my ankle outside on a bench, she encouraged me to keep breathing. As I did, I felt this amazing rush of energy throughout my whole being. The best way I can describe it is that it was like a full-body orgasm.

I stayed high all day and night. It was beautiful. It was how we're supposed to feel—full of love, light, and joy. Jacalyne told me it was very special that I could experience that, and if I could allow myself to feel that way, I could do anything. I finished the race in 40th place. Jacalyne was confused. She said there must be something we couldn't see. She hugged me and told me she loved me. I would see her back in Whistler.

The day of the 2008 Olympic opening ceremonies, I was standing in the river by Richie's house. I was surprised by my simple contentment. I had surrendered to my life. After hiring a new coach and getting off my bike for a month, I had just finished sixth at a World Cup in Canada. I knew for some reason I wasn't meant to go to the Olympics, but I also knew that bike racing wasn't over for me yet. I enjoyed the parties in Whistler and just let myself relax. Of course, I was flirting too much, and one night Richie had just had enough. He walked up to me on the dance floor, pushed me, and just turned around and walked out. I chased him out of the bar, apologizing.

We slept in separate rooms that night, and in the morning I walked to the river again to call Meadow. I told her I was finally over this relationship and wanted out. She said, "Good." I turned around to see Richie walking toward me. I was filled with a sense of panic. I knew he had an engagement ring in his pocket. I could just feel it.

I told Meadow, and she said, "What in the hell are you going to do? Haven't you been waiting for this for five years?" I told her I didn't know but would call her back. I hung up the phone and ran to the house, pretending I needed a glass of water.

I called Meadow again, and told her I didn't know if I could go back down there. I could not believe my reaction. I had been waiting for this for five years, and now I didn't know why. I had let it go, and now here it was. And it felt wrong. We'd just had a fight! I was ready to go! And now a proposal? I took a deep breath and walked down to the river. Richie was sweet and sincere, and the ring was beautiful. How could I say no to something that I thought I had so desperately wanted? So I said yes.

******

6

The End of an Era

I tried on wedding dresses and looked at venues. I called my girlfriends, and planned bachelorette and engagement parties. Richie and I couldn't decide on a place, a date, or a vibe. We were basically like we always were, but now it was just becoming glaringly obvious.

We spent a few weeks in Mexico toward the end of the fall. It was meant to be relaxing and romantic, but we were at odds over everything: money, our lack of wedding plans, our daily activities, and mostly—who we each were. And who we were not. People try to change each other all the time, and it doesn't work. I think most of our relationship was spent trying to get the other to see our own point of view.

A week into our vacation, Richie received a phone call from a friend in Whistler. He said that the story of the day was that a woman named Jacalyne had just died in a plane crash in Australia. Our friend wondered if that was our Jacalyne. It was. I was shocked. I didn't cry, though. It somehow felt oddly in line with life. Richie and I were in denial that we were dying as a couple, and Jacalyne had just died. It was a pretty definitive end to 2008.

There are no words of gratitude I could use to describe the impact Jacalyne made on my life. She was the perfect example of how, "when the student is ready, the master appears." She made it very clear to me that what I was learning and what I was living, I would pass on to others. She was the first person in my life I could open up to completely without fear of being judged. She was the first person to show me that there was a magic beyond myself that was just waiting for me to engage in. I love her, and I miss her.

***

Then 2009 rolled in, and training was on the agenda. Richie was upset that I'd chosen to race another year. I was supposed to retire after the Olympics and settle down in Whistler. I, on the other hand, was actually excited to race again. I knew nothing could be worse than last year, and it also gave me an opportunity to run away from "real life" and the state of my relationship. I was in North Carolina, and Richie was in Whistler. I decided to head back to Laguna Beach for some sunny days. I told Richie he could come if he wanted to. I was almost hoping he wouldn't, but he did.

Our apartment was small, and there was no breathing room. It was on that trip that we really both admitted we weren't happy. I cried almost every day, but training was going well. I was running a bit to break up the biking. Usually I would just hit the sand, but one day I decided to run down the main street. I saw a building that immediately grabbed my attention. Across the street was a cute little cottage with a hanging sign that said Chakra Shack. I stopped my run, looked both ways, and ran across the street.

A woman named Grace was doing psychic readings that day, and I asked to see her. I walked to the back and into her small space. Immediately I felt like my head was being lifted right off my body. She could see me. She asked what I wanted to know, and I told her. I talked about Richie and me; and I talked about my racing and my lack of control over money, drinking, and getting attention. She said, "Honey, you aren't happy. This relationship isn't about marriage. You're stuck. We have to get you un-stuck."

That may seem like a simple observation, but no one had said that to me yet. It was all about sticking it out and making it work, and hell, we were engaged! It was so amazingly liberating to admit that no, I was not happy, and yes, I was very stuck.

I'd never made the best choices in men. People say that you get what you deserve. Well, I feel like I got what I thought I deserved. I didn't think much of myself, so if I wasn't being treated very well, it didn't seem to matter. I knew all my flaws, and I was always surprised that I had enough good qualities to make up for what I lacked. At

some point in all my relationships, I realized that the men I
kept choosing really didn't like it when I was amazing. They
may have acted like they were impressed, but it seemed to
cause enormous problems when I was successful, or in any
way starting to seem "better" than they were. In many
ways, I had to dumb it down to keep the peace.

Grace worked every Friday, so I promised myself that
I'd visit every week for as long as I was in Laguna. I walked
out the door with a spring in my step. I didn't know what I
was going to do, or how I was going to do it. I just knew
that something huge had shifted in me.

I spent all my Fridays at the Chakra Shack. Grace
helped me see the beauty in life again. I thought about
what I liked, what I enjoyed, and what made me happy.
One day as I was telling her about my awful 2008 season,
she said, "The whole right side of your body is missing. I
can't see it. When you tell the story of hitting the wall at
the first World Cup, it's literally like half your body
continued on."

I was not one to argue. It felt like half my body is the
most I'd ever had. Grace called in her spiritual helpers
from the other side and began to rebuild pieces of my body.
She felt like this had happened to me lifetimes ago, and I
was just now being given the opportunity to live in a full
body this lifetime.

It's hard to fully explain to anyone else how it feels to
have experiences like this. The simplest thing I can say is
that you can feel pieces of yourself coming back. You can
sense that you've just been floating above your body,
looking in. And then you can feel when you come back in
it. I always thought that being out of my body was the
safest place to be. If I were in my body, I would feel pain,
confusion, and betrayal. If I were in my body, I would get
hurt.

But the opposite is true. When you're in your body,
you're in charge. When you're in your body, nothing else
can fill up your space. When your aura is pulled in and
your soul has a vehicle, then life is an enjoyable
experience. It's when you're living in a sort of limbo,
neither here nor there, that causes so much pain. I was

just beginning to experience all this, and it was a wonder to behold.

Every week I felt stronger and clearer. I was still with Richie, but I was more with myself than anything. I started making lists about what I wanted out of life, what I wanted out of the season, and what I wanted in a partner. I began to clarify what I liked and what I didn't, what made me feel good and what made me feel awful. I began to feel like I was the captain of my ship, even though I didn't know my destination yet. I began to feel safe being me.

The first World Cup of the year was in South Africa. I felt great, and my body and soul were happy. I spent most of the race in fourth or fifth place only to slip to sixth by the finish. The year before I'd finished in the 50s at the first World Cup, so that was like a win for me. I returned to North Carolina so I could use it as my home base for the next few races. Richie was back and forth, and I was just happy to be feeling good. With the distance between us, neither of had to be the one to say, "This isn't working."

I had another good race in Germany, where I finished 11th. I was inspired. This year was not going to be like last year—no way!

With the spring races wrapped up, I packed my bags in North Carolina and prepared for the summer in Whistler. I was going to give it my best shot. I didn't want to regret not trying at least one more time. The first few weeks were beautiful. The sun was out, and I was relaxed about training and racing. I decided to enjoy the bliss between life challenges and not address the state of my relationship with Richie. I think we were both happy to just let it be.

Given my dismal results from last season, my team wanted me to do some "fun" races to appease sponsors and take the pressure off myself. The next scheduled event for me was a Super D race in Ashland, Oregon. Super D is a mix of downhill skills and cross-country fitness, and the tracks are usually between 30 and 40 minutes long. The mix of skills meant that downhillers and cross-country racers would be there, creating a more fun and less stressful environment than the World Cup series. At the end of the 2008 season, I was just happy that sponsors wanted me for anything. Now, though, there was nothing I wanted to do less. The sponsors pay you, and you do what they ask, so I tried to psych myself up for the task at hand.

I remember talking to Richie on the phone in the Portland airport. All of a sudden I was sad again. I wasn't in Whistler, I didn't want to go where I was going, and where were Richie and I going anyway? He mentioned that a couple we knew was expecting a baby. This made me even sadder. Through my tears, I asked, "Richie, what are we doing?"

"I don't know, Willow," he replied. "I'm just trying to be happy." We ended the call, and I just sat on the floor, waiting for the flight to Ashland. I tried to get it together so people wouldn't ask me what was wrong, but it was hard to suppress how I felt. This time, I couldn't lie to myself.

I arrived in Ashland depressed and quiet. I just wanted to get this over with and get home. I went to greet the sponsors and other racers on the team at the cabin above mine. I took a seat in the corner and tried to act like I was present. Then, through the door walked a regal figure. Standing 6'3" with a shock of blond hair, arresting blue eyes, and a body like a Greek god, he was hard to miss. I realized that it was Myles Rockwell, the former downhill world champion. I also knew he'd gotten into some trouble with the law for growing pot plants a few years back. I wondered what he was doing here. He walked across the room to introduce himself, but I just stayed on the floor as he extended his hand. He told me later me that his first thoughts were, "I didn't know she was so pretty", and "she looks so sad."

I didn't think much about our meeting. In fact, I stayed quiet most of the night. I was hardly eating and obviously distressed. Myles was giving me a hard time at dinner, encouraging me to eat "one more papadum" at the Indian restaurant we all went to. The crew headed out to see a band, and I went back to get some sleep. As I was leaving, I heard Myles say, "Now that is a gluten-free ass." I rolled my eyes to myself and reveled in my own misery.

The next day we headed out to practice the track. I started the day feeling pretty much the same as before. Myles kept trying to get me to talk, and I kept looking at him with a mixture of irritation and amazement. But he was quite persistent. Midway down our first run, everything changed. We were waiting for the whole group to catch up, and Myles was nowhere to be seen. He finally rolled up with a bloody arm and a desperate look in his eyes. I recognized that look. I had felt that look. It was a look of a soul who could no longer bear to be tortured by self or others. I knew how those crashes felt, and I immediately wanted to comfort him. I looked at his arm and offered some sympathetic words. I told him I had some magic bandages back at the house and that I would help him out later. All of a sudden, I liked the guy. All of a sudden, the woods seemed more magical. As we exited the foggy trail and headed into the sun at the park below, I felt like engaging with the world again.

***

Myles and I started up a conversation that would last the rest of the weekend. As I opened up, so did he. We were in a vortex of inspiration, feeding off each other's vibes. The rest of our group felt amazing, too. We were channeling energy like it was our life's purpose. I didn't know what was happening, but I knew I just wanted to be near him. I felt electric. I felt real. This didn't have to do with drinking or partying; this was just me on my bike in the woods. I thought I felt so great because of the trail or the kombucha or the great food at the hippie co-op. I didn't think it was possible for me to feel like this for no reason.

We made sure to sit next to each other at dinners, and talked about parallel universes in between shuttle runs. I mentioned my recent fascination with reptilians and shape-shifters, and Myles acted like that was as normal as talking about where we went to school. I wasn't used to that! One night as we were walking behind the group, laughing and vibing high, he reached over and grabbed my hand. I actually didn't remember this until months later. It just seemed like the most natural thing in the world.

On our last afternoon in Ashland, I looked over at him from my bike and said, "Myles, I am really going to miss you." He told me he was going to miss me, too, and I should call him sometime if I was ever in Durango,

Colorado. I told him I would. A few hours later on the deck with the crew, I was saying my good-byes. As I hugged Myles, I looked up at him with total surprise.

"Oh my God!" I exclaimed. "I just remembered I had the biggest crush on you when I was 16!"

He laughed and said, "Oh, that's sweet. You should have talked to me!" I told him I was nowhere near the same person I was now when I was 16, and he wouldn't have even noticed me. I turned around to walk back to my cabin, but a minute later I was running back up the stairs to Myles's room. I walked straight in and gave him the biggest hug I could. We didn't say anything. After a minute, he asked, "What are you going to do?" I told him I didn't know. I said good-bye one more time and walked out the door. I was sad, but I also felt alive.

***

I was on my way back to Whistler the next day. But the closer I got, the less alive I felt. On the long drive from Vancouver, the tears began to fall. Five minutes from home I had to pull over to the side of the road. I couldn't breathe, I couldn't drive. I picked up my phone and called Myles. He answered. I told him where I was and what I was feeling. I told him that I'd had the greatest weekend, and I wasn't sure what was happening to me. Myles let me know that he'd just come out of an awful divorce and that he was in no place for a relationship. He told me he was "damaged goods." So am I, I thought to myself. So am I.

Myles didn't want to break up my engagement, but he did tell me to pay attention to my feelings.

"If you don't want to go home, Willow, it may not be your home. Be honest with yourself if you can." I thanked him for his advice and hung up the phone. I drove the last five minutes as slowly as I could.

I told Richie about my fun times, and I also told him about meeting Myles. I didn't tell him how much I liked Myles, but I did say I had a good time. I told him I was suddenly sad being back in Whistler again, and he told me it was impossible to feel that great all the time. I called Grace and told her what was going on in my life. She told me that it didn't matter if Myles and I were going to be together or not . . . he had saved me. He'd given me the gift of being able to be in my aliveness, and now I would settle for nothing less. She told me I knew what I needed to do, and I was finally just going to have to do it.

I resisted, of course. I tried to get on with my life. I tried to be happy. I didn't cry. One of my eyes was red and infected from holding all my emotions in. My body was rebelling against my denial. I was making scones one day, and I just burst into tears. I let the batter get saturated with my pain, and I just let it out!

For some reason I felt like listening to Madonna again. I went for a bike ride, and as the song "Frozen" was playing, a robin flew beside me for the longest minute of my life. The lyrics to the song are now a tattoo on my arm. Basically, that song encouraged me to fly away. When I got home, I went to my computer and looked up the meaning behind "robin" as an animal totem. I found that it symbolizes the "spread of new growth," and "belief in yourself as you move forward." As a result, "Obstacles will fall by the wayside if you do, and confrontations will be for show only."

I stared at the computer screen with a mix of disbelief and awe. What more did I need to know? How much clearer could it be? I called my coach and told him I was leaving Whistler to go home to North Carolina, and this time for good. He was worried about me making this decision in the middle of the season, but I assured him that I would slowly die if I didn't. He didn't think North Carolina was the place for me to go. Too many people, too many questions. He told me he had a place for me to stay in Durango, Colorado. It was small, but it was free.

Wasn't Myles from Durango? It was too weird. I told my coach I would take him up on his offer, and I booked my plane ticket for two days later. That was enough time for me. I had nothing in Whistler but clothing that I was sick of anyway.

It wasn't an easy couple of days. I was cried out, but it was Richie's turn to be emotional. But just like the robin predicted, it was all for show. I left the night before my flight to stay with a friend in Vancouver. It was too much to ask from either Richie or me to spend any more time together. It was over, and we needed to be apart.

It took me two days to get to Durango. I can't remember why, but I had to stay in a hotel. Michael Jackson and Farrah Fawcett died that day, and it was the only thing on TV. I looked around the hotel room and thought to myself, "What on earth do I think I'm doing?" I called Meadow, and she encouraged me to stay strong. I couldn't sleep that night.

I finally arrived in Durango. My coach, Rick Crawford, sent his son to pick me up. We stopped at a health-food store, and I picked up a few things. Rick's son took me to my small, sparse apartment. I thanked him and put my bags on the floor. I had just moved from a mansion to a dump, but I was free. This was my space. This was my life.

******

7

Love Versus Fear

My coach showed me the rides around town and organized training rides for me with other racers. I soaked up the sun, and I soaked in the river. I didn't have a car, so I rode my bike or walked everywhere. An afternoon rain shower usually fell on me after my trip to the local health-food store. I let it wash away my anxieties and cleanse my fears.

The mountain-bike community in Durango embraced me right away. Meg and Todd Wells introduced me to their crew and invited me to barbeques and social events. I had never felt more at home, and I had just moved there.

After about a week in Durango, I got up the nerve to call Myles. I didn't know what he'd think about my arrival, but I had nothing to lose by calling him. He'd already told me that he was damaged goods and not looking for a relationship. I thought maybe we could at least ride together. I didn't know if I wanted a relationship either, but I did want to feel good, and I did want to have fun.

I left a message for him and continued on with my new social life. He called while I was on a bike ride with my coach.

"Are you really in Durango?" he asked.

"Yes, I'm here, just riding around town." He was on the couch watching motocross and seemed quite content to stay there. He invited me over the next evening for a drink. I thought that was pretty promising news! I hung up the phone and started thinking about what to wear, or not wear, the next night.

Needless to say, we picked up right where we left off. Except this time it wasn't wrong to admit that we were lusting after each other. I didn't know if we were going anywhere as a couple, but I didn't care. He made me feel good, he said amazing things, and I just wanted to be naked with him as soon as possible. And so did he. We hooked up again the next night, and then I didn't hear from him for a week. I left a message, but only one. It was a challenging week for me. I had to get to the point where I was okay if he never called me again. I hadn't come to Durango for Myles; I'd come for myself. For the first time in my adult life, I'd made a decision to move on with my life without the security of another boyfriend in the wings.

After a week of heartache, I decided to get on with my life. I went on a date with a guy in town, and a mountain-bike ride with him a day later. He fell for me fast, and that scared me, but at least I'd tried! I got my hair done and sprayed on a tan. I was going to get out in the world, damn it, even if it killed me.

I remember the day I was walking down the main street feeling so good. I looked good, I was fine on my own, and I was feeling great on my bike. The local bike shop called to say my Gary Fisher cruiser bike had arrived and I should come pick it up. I wondered how long of a walk it would be to 32nd Street. Maybe I should take the bus. I looked across the street, and Myles was walking out of a government building. My heart skipped a beat. Or five.

I called his name, and when he saw me, he seemed both surprised and happy. He ran across the street and we smiled at each other. The air seemed rarefied and full of gold dust. I wasn't thinking about why he hadn't called me or anything else. I knew how I looked and I knew how I felt, and I knew that Myles must feel intoxicated, too. I just wanted to live in the moment.

He gave me a ride to the bike shop, and before I went in to pick up my cruiser, we chatted at the back of his truck. He apologized for not calling, but said he'd been busy with his son and had a pretty intense life right now. I told him it was okay and that we should hang out again sometime. He agreed, and I decided that he would call me if he wanted to. And he did. We rode mountain bikes Monday after work and then rode our cruiser bikes to dinner. Our lives became an open book very quickly, and our hearts decided that love was worth the risk of being hurt again. From that moment on, we were together.

We kept our relationship a secret for a while. Myles wanted to protect me from too many questions in the bike world, and I couldn't agree more. We reveled in our bliss, and found the time to hang out under trees by the river and have long dinners on his patio. We drank life-changing wine and cried because it felt safe to do so. He told me about his dramas and struggles, and I shared mine with him. We only had a few weeks together before I headed off for a month of races. He'd never seen me race, but he had seen me ride. He told me I could win anything I wanted to. He built me up in every way he could. Not because he was trying to, but because it was natural for him to want people to feel good.

Myles was brought up knowing that he was loved and that it was important for him to love himself. Our foundations were fundamentally different, and he could see that my lack of love for myself was my biggest, scariest hurdle. To Myles, love is all there is. And he's right. Everything that matters comes from love. As my mentor Dr. Leonard Laskow writes: "All human endeavor is either an expression of love or a cry for love." Whatever we want or think we need, we seek because we think we will feel better in the having of it. What I was beginning to see through Myles was that without love to start with, those things, experiences, or relationships will never fill the void.

I soaked up his words. I'd been living in a love desert, and Myles saw beauty in me that I had yet to see in myself. He saw my soul, and he saw my heart. I was used to only showing my physical body and hiding the rest, because it scared me too much. In my opinion, there was an unexplored dungeon of demons within me. Myles helped me see that the things that scared me the most, and that I wanted to do the least, were exactly the issues I needed to address in order to heal.

As we sat under a tree a few days before my departure, Myles said to me, "Let's go ahead and put it out there in the universe that it's okay for you to win at least one of these races." I promised myself that I would follow through on that statement. I wanted to make him proud.

The trip started off as planned. I finished fifth at the World Cup in Mt. St. Anne, Canada, and seventh at the next World Cup in Bromont, also in Canada, despite getting a flat front tire. I had the fastest lap of the day and led the first lap. I flew through the technical sections like they didn't exist. I had the confidence, I had the skills, and I was fast. The momentum continued, and I finished second at the National Race in Vermont, a handful of seconds off the lead.

The next week was hard on me, I clearly remember. Bit by bit, pain was leaking toward the surface. I cried a lot, and tried to clear it as best I could. At this point, it was still so confusing as to what was so painful; but whatever it was, it usually just felt completely overwhelming. One thing I remember clearly is the panic I felt when I thought of Myles knowing everything about me. He wouldn't see me the same, and my sparkle would fade. In my mind, I wasn't worthy of anyone's unconditional love.

My credit-card bill was huge, and I decided that not only did I need to win the next race in New York because I'd promised I would, but I needed the money. It wasn't huge money, but $3,000 would pay off the mattress I was sleeping on and the rent and deposit on my new apartment. It was my race, and no one needed it more. I won, but I won from a place of pain. I had two flat tires that day, but it didn't stop me. I had to win. I kept telling myself up every climb, "This is your money, this is your race, no one is suffering like you, no one wants it more than you."

I truly believe that no one did want it more. I fell in the dirt at the finish line and made dirt angels. I wouldn't say I was happy. I would call it relief. Relief from what, I wasn't sure. Maybe it was relief from the voices in my head that were telling me I had to win, or needed the money, or couldn't go back to Durango without a victory. For one night at least, those voices had to shut up.

I arrived in Durango fresh from victory and completely insecure about my life. Myles and I had really only spent a few weeks together before being apart for a month. I felt distant and spacey, unable to let him engage me. He spent the evening letting me warm up to him. I finally relaxed and remembered that he was a good guy, that I was safe, I wasn't at the start line, and I could let my guard down. We had ten days before I left for the World Championships in Australia, and we made the most of it.

It's hard to remember every detail, because most of those days felt like a lucid dream. I found myself explaining to Myles just recently that before I met him, my life felt two-dimensional. I saw myself as a series of paper cut-out dolls lined up all over the globe. I couldn't really relate to any of those "me's."That's because I never really was any of those Willows. Since we'd met, though, life had become vivid and bright. I saw the shadows and light in my memories; and I felt solid, not paper thin.

I opened up more and more to Myles, and every time I was vulnerable, I was rewarded tenfold. It took me a long time to trust people, but with Myles, the process was remarkably rapid. He'd been through many trying life experiences as well, and he could relate. His challenges seemed to come from the outside world, while mine came from within. Challenges are challenges, though, and his warrior was seeing my "warrioress."

***

Myles seemed to have an uncanny knack for getting into trouble with the law. After his bike-racing years were over, his addiction to adrenaline kept him on the local police radar. A few years before he retired, he began a relationship with a very intense young woman. It was easy for him to overlook the warning signs, as he was traveling most of the year. But once he stopped traveling, he realized he needed to get out of the relationship. He began the process of ending things with her, and packed up his truck with his bikes and dogs to celebrate the end of his career with a solo road trip. While on this trip, his girlfriend called him. She was pregnant. He panicked, of course, but wanted to do the right thing. He promised to try and make the relationship work for the sake of his unborn child. On May 31, 2003, Myles' son was born.

Myles wanted a way to provide for his new family without struggling in a nine-to-five job. He began to cultivate 52 marijuana plants in his basement with the intent to sell. His girlfriend created drama, given any opportunity. Her instability grew increasingly worse after the birth of their son. Myles was arrested once when she

57

called the cops claiming he'd hit her. A few months later, the cops showed up with a summons, requiring the ex to appear in court regarding the allegations. A few hours later, they showed up again to bust Myles for growing marijuana. They'd suspected something was going on when they'd visited his house earlier that day. Myles was also charged with violating the protection order placed on him by his ex. He wasn't even allowed to be at his own house. He had to plead guilty in the domestic-violence case in order to receive a lesser punishment on the marijuana charge. He settled for harassment and cultivation, and spent a month in jail. He was now labeled a wife beater and a felon.

I knew the truth, though. I could see it, and most of all, I could feel it. Myles was the kindest person I'd ever met, and I trusted him. We respected each other, as well as what we had each been through. That mutual respect allowed us to create an atmosphere for divine mutual healing.

We spent more time at the river and went on easy rides together. Myles encouraged me to forgive my parents for not knowing a better way to teach me, and we cried together about him missing his son. He had just finalized a nasty divorce with the mother of his son in December. They had never married, but because of Colorado's definition of Common Law Marriage, a lengthy process of separation was required.

Myles agreed to settle affairs through mediation rather than bringing his ex to court. Since it was Myles who had instigated the separation, she wouldn't sign the divorce papers until she was satisfied. Myles gave her the house they were living in and the bar they owned together. He allowed her the majority of the parenting time and also gave her a substantial amount of money in child support. Myles trusted that she would allow him to see his son on the days they'd both agreed on. Although the divorce liberated him from her everyday mood swings, the ordeal was far from over.

When his ex found out we were dating, she withheld their son from Myles. He finally realized that his faith in her was blind. He was going to need the court's help to determine and enforce the parenting time. He reluctantly began to file the necessary paperwork. As a father, he helped me see that although mistakes are bound to be a part of parenthood, there's an undercurrent of love that will always exist. He told me I should call my Mom and Dad before I boarded the plane to Australia, and just tell them I forgave them. The details didn't matter at this point, but the forgiveness would free me up.

Myles took me on a long motorcycle ride, and I just leaned into his back and let the scenery pass by. It felt nice to finally trust someone, especially a man. Later that night we were getting fired up about the World Championships. Myles knew I could win, and his belief was contagious. I started to believe it, too. I started to let myself imagine being great. I started to let myself feel excited and inspired. No one in the bike world would have picked me for a medal that year, let alone a win. But it didn't matter. We both knew how much I'd held myself back through the years. Our belief in me was the only thing that mattered at that moment.

Myles left the room for a minute and came back with his World Championship jersey and gold medal.

"Take your clothes off," he told me. "Let's put this on you." He slipped the jersey over my head and put the medal around my neck.

"Look at you!" he exclaimed. "You are the World Champion!" He told me to put my hands in the air and act like I'd won. It was harder than I thought to show such exuberance, but I gave it my best shot. He encouraged me to not hold back and to really be happy. He took some photos that he promised he'd e-mail when I arrived in Australia.

Myles packed my bike with care and intention. I packed my suitcases with hope and expectation. I boarded the plane and wished for as much sleep as possible.

I took it easy when I first arrived. I didn't have much physical training to do; I just had to keep my mind and spirit on track. I had an awful crash the first time I rode the course, and the next day my left shoulder and neck were in complete spasm. I had to spend most of the day in bed. My injury was a gateway to some form of emotional release, and I worked through it as best I could.

I let myself cry about missing Jacalyne. I was in her country, after all. I let myself cry about my childhood wounds, and I admitted to myself that I felt guilty about moving on from Richie so quickly. I decided to call him and update him on my life. It was a sad but beneficial phone call. I felt lighter the more baggage I cleared. I knew that the lighter my load, the easier the hills would seem.

Myles sent me the photos of me in the rainbow jersey, as well as an e-mail full of praise and encouragement. I called him the day before my race, and he hesitantly told me that he'd spent the night in jail.

"For what, baby?" I asked. I couldn't believe it. I already knew he'd spent time in jail before. I thought those times were over, and I was confused. He told me that he'd finally gotten to spend time with his son, and he texted his ex to get permission to retrieve a few last items from her garage. She told him it was no problem to collect his things. Included in his belongings were bikes from his glory days as well as his grandfather's antique shotgun. She wasn't home when he picked up his belongings.

Later that night, the cops showed up at his house. He'd been accused of "ramshackling" her garage as well as possessing a weapon. Myles was a convicted felon due to the pot case, and he wasn't allowed to have a gun. Never mind that his grandfather's gun had no bullets, didn't work, and was a family heirloom. To the cops, a gun was a gun. A restraining order was placed on Myles, prohibiting him from being around his ex, and more important, his son.

Myles was released on bail, and was sentenced to probation until a court date was set. He eventually had to plead guilty to trespassing so he could receive a deferred judgment on possessing his grandfather's shotgun. Once again, he had to admit to a crime he didn't commit in order to save himself from the legal system. He was allowed only one weekly visit with his son until family investigators compiled a full report on the case. For a few hours every week, he tried to salvage his relationship with his son under the suspicious and watchful eyes of the counselors at the Family Center.

I listened to the story and tried not to think too far ahead. Myles apologized but said he wanted me to know the truth. We were trying not to hide our faults and our messes from each other, and I respected that. He told me I was the best rider in the world, the most beautiful girl, and his best friend. He told me to go win tomorrow, and to do it for myself. I went to bed that night full of nervous anticipation. I had never started a World Championship race expecting to win. It was an entirely new experience.

I woke up feeling relaxed and purposeful. My start number was 11, and that was a great sign for me. I'd been seeing 11's everywhere I looked for years. I remember the stillness of the air that morning, and the way the sun was softly sending warmth my way. When I lined up, I told my mechanic not to worry—I wouldn't be seeing him until the finish line.

The gun went off, and not one minute into the race, a huge pileup occurred. I managed to come out unscathed, but a large group of girls were in front of me leading up to the single track. I took a deep breath and just stayed calm. I was here to win, and this wouldn't rattle me. Bit by bit, I picked off riders. I saw the 2007 World Champion Irina Kalentieva get off her bike with a chain problem. One heavy hitter out, I thought. I continued my chase and finished Lap 1 in the top five.

All of my best races, like all of my best memories, are hard to explain in detail. What it always comes down to is a feeling. It's like floating above yourself and being totally "in" yourself at the same time—a feeling of pure connection to source, and the body you inhabit. A genuine flow of energy and magic. An orgasmic and cosmic experience. That feeling is what I remember most that day. I remember never looking behind me, and I remember orchestrating the race in my mind . . . then watching my body execute the instructions perfectly.

I had certain visualizations for certain parts of the course. On one particular climb, I envisioned that I was riding on a rainbow carpet that was being pulled to the top by Myles, my family, and my friends. I literally felt no pain

61

on that climb. It felt flat. In fact, on the second-to-last lap, I made a pivotal move by dropping the current Olympic Gold Medalist Sabine Spitz. People complimented me afterward on my strategy and strength at that particular moment. Truth be told, I did not even know she was behind me. I was in my own universe, racing my own race.

I headed into the last lap in second place, 17 seconds down on the leader, Lene Byberg from Norway. I put my head down to catch her and felt an abundance of energy flow into my legs. Midway up the first climb, I heard yelling behind me. Irina had made an incredible comeback from her earlier mechanical issue, and was riding like she was possessed. She passed me, and I tried to stay on her wheel. But I couldn't. I watched her for a second as she charged up the climb, and then I refocused my energy. Anything can happen in mountain biking, and you never give up until the end. I was alone in the Bronze Medal position, and I was enjoying every moment. I chased as hard as I could, and I smiled the whole last lap. I knew the Bronze was mine, and the feeling I'd been carrying with me was Gold Medal material.

I cruised into the finish line with time to blow kisses to the crowd and to savor the moment. Irina passed Lene for the victory, and I finished 52 seconds behind. Time slowed way down, and my dreamlike trance carried me through the podium ceremony, interviews, and congratulatory hugs. I felt how I always wanted to feel, and I didn't want to come down from the high. This feeling was the high that athletes chase. The Bronze Medal was a high in itself, but the trancelike state of my race and my existence was the true drug. It made up for all the suffering and pain.

I called Myles, and we talked about the feeling. He knew exactly how slow time was moving for me at the moment, and he encouraged me to savor it. He knew as well as I that it wouldn't last for long. He was beyond excited for my performance; he'd watched the race live on the internet. He said he was screaming so loud at the screen that he had to shut the doors and windows so the neighbors wouldn't get upset. I couldn't wait to be back in his arms. He was the one person in my life who knew exactly how much work I'd done to allow this to happen.

I didn't want to party that night. I didn't want to ruin how I felt. I had some wine, but it didn't taste that great. I was starting to come down from the buzz, and to be honest, things seemed a little depressing. As good as I'd felt, it seemed like a lot of effort for such brief glory. I'd been chasing the top for most of my life, and now "almost there" didn't feel good enough. I began to wonder if I would be feeling complete if I'd won. I slept that night, but I didn't dream.

Back in Durango, I was greeted with a welcome-home banner and lots of hugs. But Myles was the only one I wanted to see. It felt so good to be in the arms of understanding. He knew I was happy, and he also knew that I was left slightly unsatisfied. That's how dreams of glory affect you. If you're not the best, there's room for self-torture.

Looking back at my life now, I wonder if I held myself just below the best just to keep the self-sabotage close to my side. It was an old, familiar friend—one I wasn't ready to part with just quite yet. As I unpacked, I put the Bronze Medal on my shabby closet door and just looked at it. It may have slightly changed how other people saw me, but it didn't change how I saw me. Not in the slightest.

I spent the fall riding my mountain bike, and slowly but surely drifting into heavy drinking. I got a tattoo on my arm, I shopped, I danced, I caused a scene, I was fun. I remember one morning Myles stopped by my house, and he was practically begging me to stop partying. He couldn't go out at all because of the probation, and he honestly told me he was beginning to feel resentful. I was surprised by my reaction. Usually when boyfriends would call me out on my behavior, I would become defensive. This time I listened, and I actually agreed. My behavior was getting out of control. I could feel myself right on the edge. It felt nice to have someone want to pull me back instead of egging me on.

I listened, and I tried, but drinking was the only way to keep the past that wanted to surface down where I thought it belonged. I was uncomfortable at night without a steady flow of wine, and I didn't know how to engage fully with others unless I was under the influence. In short, I felt that the sober me wasn't good enough. Fall turned into winter, and the snow was falling. Myles and I spent lots of days catching powder turns and enjoying my respite from racing. My family came to Durango for Christmas break, and a whole new layer of my psyche was soon to unravel.

I love my family, but the truth is, being around them would trigger huge layers of emotional trauma. Our bodies hold memories and reactions even when we're not aware of them. Our seven-layer auric body system holds imprints of beliefs (true or false), experiences, emotions, and behaviors. It's like a blueprint of where we've been in our lives. Certain situations or people cause certain emotional and behavioral responses. The body is just acting in the way it has been taught to react. When all this is unknown and the triggers remain unconscious, it can lead to some pretty traumatic feelings flooding through one's system. I had called on powerful medicine, and even though I didn't feel ready, I was ready to begin to clear my blueprint. Healing isn't easy, and this was no exception.

With my family in town, I felt tense, on edge, and on display. I could never really relax around them, I always felt like I had to show that I was okay—that I was healthy, happy, and content. Even if I wasn't. It had been a game of charades for as long as I could remember. Better not to talk about anything real and just focus on trying to have fun. I agree with this concept to a point, but when you have real wounds that you need to heal in this lifetime, avoidance only causes more pain.

After about a week of "faking it," I started to crumble. It was as if an explosion was building up inside me and I could feel the pressure valve about to pop. My parents left, and my brother stayed to hang out for a night with Myles and me. We went to the bars in Durango, and of course I drank to keep the explosion at bay. This technique works until it doesn't work anymore. The dam will break eventually whether you like it or not. At one point I went to stand up on the bar, and Myles said "Willow, get down. I don't know who this is, but it isn't you." He told me later he could tell right then that "something" or "someone" had taken over my energy field. He could see it in my eyes, and he could feel it around me.

What I know now is that drinking causes cracks to form in your energy field. The more you drink, the more cracks occur. What you feel to be a "buzz" is just lack of form in the aura around you. When you're weak, vulnerable, or far removed from your body, you create space for darker energies to enter. It makes sense that darker energies would be hanging around a bar. Think of all the depressed and lonely people who go there to drink away their troubles. Of course, you can also drink and party just for fun, but I do believe that most people who drink heavily are trying to keep the dam from bursting.

Given my getting-on-the-bar antics, it was apparent that it was time to go home. As soon as we got to my little house, I just lost it. Me, plus the darker energies, were depressed beyond belief. I couldn't hold it in anymore; the dam had broken. I've experienced a lot of these types of episodes, but this one had a more real and raw edge to it. My brother and Myles were asking what was wrong, and I just told them all of it—all the details about my childhood trauma and confusion and the residual body/mind issues I'd dealt with throughout my life up to this point. I'm sure my brother was shocked to hear it all, and I know Myles had never heard it quite like that. I'd always tried to be composed and rational when it came to talking about my past or the things that were coming to the surface. They just let me cry.

The next morning I was mortified, of course. Not only I was furious at myself for drinking so much, but I realized that the words I'd spoken could not be taken back. It was all out there on the table. And I was not okay. No amount of apologizing was going to change the fact that I had a lot of work to do. I knew it, Myles knew it, and now my brother knew it, too. No Bronze Medal or new pair of shoes was going to fix me. Unless I faced my demons, I would destroy myself.

I guess I would call this time in my life "rock bottom with awareness." My previous rock bottoms were just so confusing that I didn't know what to do. Mostly, I would just ride them out and hope the upswing wouldn't be that far off. What was happening now, though, was that I was admitting that my past had actually happened, and that it really hurt.

When traumatic events are suppressed and kept silent, it makes you question yourself constantly. What really happened? Was it really wrong? Was it my fault in some way? Is it possible that it really messed me up this much? The world becomes gray, and black-and-white answers are nowhere to be found. Events were now becoming real to me, and I was about to relive them in order to release them.

Myles came over to my house and offered his full support. He held me, and let me know that it was safe for me to heal. He wasn't going anywhere. For the first time in my life, I felt like it actually was safe to heal. I'd just let every bit of mess out of my body, and he still loved and supported me. I will never forget how grateful and lucky I felt that morning. I told Myles I wouldn't drink for at least a few days. I would start 2010 right. I would face this shit, and I would deal with whatever came up.

That evening, Myles offered to use a magnetic massager on my back. My right lower back in particular felt like there was a knife in it. This area of my back had been plaguing me for years. I learned later, with the help of my shaman, that the pain was from the guilt and rejection I'd felt when my family strongly disapproved of my decision to be with Richie. This was hidden from view at the time, though, and all I knew was that it hurt. After about five minutes, my whole body started shaking. Then I started to cry. I couldn't stop.

Myles asked what he should do, as he was starting to freak out. I told him to just stay on my back because something was draining out of me, and I didn't want to stop it. I can't remember how long the crying lasted, but the body-shaking was going to last for another year at least. My auric fields were doing their best to shake off the pain even though I didn't know it yet. The spasms were pretty intense. I would be sitting still and my head would jerk back or my arm would fling out to the side. Totally involuntary and really embarrassing. I just told myself to let it out, let it out, let it out.

One night I was lying in bed, and the sweat just started pouring off of me. And I became terrified. Not scared, terrified. I sat up in bed, and I could have sworn that the man from church who wrote me that terrible letter years ago was walking down the road toward me. I was hallucinating, yes, but I was also reliving how I'd felt whenever he was near me. I started shaking again and just lay down on the bed and told myself that it would pass. It felt similar to the time I'd come down from cocaine, only this time there were no drugs and no alcohol. I was detoxing from terror. This detox would last the rest of the year.

As was the case with my entire healing process, it would only be until much later that I would discover why the fear would be kicked into full gear. Fear is a powerful drug. Fear feeds off fear and creates a reality to match the illusion. Fear attracts dark energies, entities, and other fearful people. Fear is the most powerful illusion there is.

Traumatic events also rob you of your animal medicine, or power. You can spend a lifetime operating way below your potential in a fear-based reality. Neurologically, your mind has trouble distinguishing from real or perceived danger. In this state, everything is scary, and everything is about to get you.

The year 2010 was the end of a cycle for me. Later that year I would be introduced to Stargazer Li. Her astrology and calendar is based on Mayan time cycles, numbers, and symbols; I discovered that 2010 was my last year in a 13-year cycle of being in the night. I was about to become a star, but the night would get darker first.

******

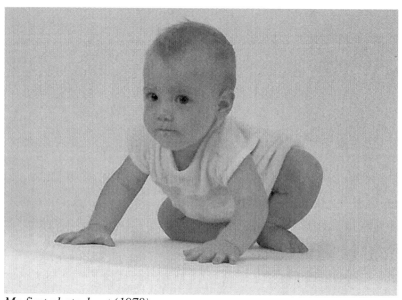

My first photoshoot (1978)

Age 7 or 8

Meadow and I at Fletcher Academy, age 14

Jacalyne and I in Tulum, Mexico, Fall of 2007

Richie and I in Tulum Mexico, December 2008

Winning the Bronze Medal in Canberra, Australia, 2009. Photo by Rob Jones.

Leading the World Cup, Spring of 2010. Photo by Rob Jones.

Cyclepassion calendar photo by Daniel Geiger.

75

Cyclepassion calendar photo by Daniel Geiger.

*Winning Bronze again at the 2010 World Championships. Photo by
Frank Bodenmueller.*

*A kiss from Myles after the podium presentation at the 2010 World
Championships. Photo by Frank Bodenmueller.*

Engagement photos with Myles, 3 months pregnant.

In my TREK World Racing Jersey, 3 months pregnant. Shot by Hailey King.

7 months pregnant, shot by Candace Cross.

Raven Starr was born December 31st at 4:04 pm.

8
The Middle of the Night

As my body continued to dispel trauma, my legs turned to cement. It was time to train, but I couldn't. In fact, I could hardly move. I felt like someone had a voodoo doll and was sticking needles in me constantly. I decided to stay off my bike and just cross-country ski. I couldn't handle feeling that terrible on my bike.

By mid-February, Myles convinced me to attempt to ride. I tried to hang on his wheel for a two-hour ride and hated every second of it. Every second. I finished that ride and remember walking into my house, throwing my helmet on the floor, and dramatically falling to the ground. I think Myles wanted to laugh at me, but one look at my face showed that I was truly suffering. I had no energy, no legs, and wasn't having any fun. The first races were in mid-March, and I hadn't even begun to ride my bike yet. I tried to shake it off and thought for sure I'd feel better next time. But I felt worse. I continued to force myself for a week until I actually couldn't push myself anymore.

I remember it was a totally crappy day, and I thought I would ski for an hour and ride for an hour. No big deal. Or so I thought.

I got on the bike to follow Myles out and back on a flat road. He dropped me in the first five minutes. It felt like I was climbing the Alps. He kept circling around back to me, and I was getting more upset every time. I tried to explain that it wasn't like I wasn't trying, I was! I was completely freaked out. It was exactly how I'd felt during every damn race in 2008. I couldn't take that kind of torture again. I begged Myles to just let us turn around, and after a few more minutes, we did. I swear, I could barely make it back to the car. Myles watched me cry and tried to offer soothing words, saying that surely I'd feel better soon. I wasn't convinced. I decided to call Grace. It had been quite a while.

Grace asked me for details about the recent events in my life. I filled her in on the slide back into heavy drinking, and the stress the family visit had caused. I told her about the night sweats and terrors, and the body shakes and tremors. She read my aura and could feel that I felt "tapped" and drained—like someone had sucked the blood right out of me. She felt an entity attached, and let me know that my drinking and slide into depression had created an opening for this to happen. Dark attracts dark. I had disrespected myself and my body, and I had to reboot again. We scheduled a time over the weekend to perform an entity extraction. I told Myles, and he didn't seem surprised.

Driving home from snowboarding over the weekend, Myles casually asked me, "So what time is the exorcism?" I will always be so thankful for the casual way in which he approached the situation. He wasn't scared of the darker side of human nature; he knew that within all of us exists the potential to self-destruct or to totally transform. I laughed, and relaxed about it myself.

As I lay on my bed later that weekend, Grace went to work over the phone. She found a gargoyle on my left clavicle and began to talk encouragingly to it to coax it to leave. A happier place existed for this entity, and my fear and depression would no longer feed it. She had her "helpers" assist in the gargoyle moving up and out of my body, my aura, and the house. I instantly felt relief, and energy flooded through me for the first time in months. She placed sentries around the corners of the house and the property, and assured me that Myles and I were safe.

I came out of the room and was beaming. Myles remarked, "That looks like it went well!"

"It did!" I told him. "It's time to train."

I had just one month before my first race, and not a moment to spare. The body tremors were still occurring, but they were less like seizures and more like spastic jerks. I tried acupuncture to help calm my nerves and assist with the reprogramming of my cells. I'd been though a lot over the years, and my body needed to catch up with my soul. I

had an awareness that my body was shaking off what no
longer served it, and I let it do what it needed to do.

I felt strong in my training, and confident that quality
over quantity would do the trick. Most people spend
months getting ready to race a World Cup season. I put
that thought out of my mind and made every ride count. I
didn't waste time putting in long, slow miles. Instead, I
latched on to the back of Myles's wheel. He was content to
sacrifice himself so I could stay out of the wind and
practice getting used to the pain of pushing just beyond my
comfort zone. Many times I wanted to shout, "Slow down!"
But I didn't. I knew I was being blessed with exactly the
training my body and soul responded to. Training with
purpose. This year, I wanted to win.

My first race was a National in California. I finished
third in the cross-country and won the short track, which
seemed like an easy ride to the park. I knew the speed was
there. Then I was off to Guatemala to race the Pan
American Championships. I attacked from the gun and
won easily. Next was the Sea Otter Classic in California. I
managed to get sloshed on red wine at an event two days
before the races. I was completely hungover the day before
the short-track race. To punish myself, I decided to attack
from the gun and practically kill myself. I didn't care about
a win here; I was thinking about the World Cup in Great
Britain the next weekend. I attacked, and shattered the
field. I messed up a few times in a muddy section and let
the win escape me. But I didn't care. I had absolved some
of the guilt of my drinking excess, and now I could give
myself a break. In the cross-country I had no legs. I could
hardly hold on for fourth place.

On my way home for two days before my Europe trip,
the panic began to sink in. Old issues with my body began
to surface, and I started to feel the usual discord settling
in. I didn't have time for this. I had to race the first World
Cup of the year the next weekend. It felt like my body was
attacking me, and that it would betray me at any minute. I
hadn't trained enough, I drank too much, and I didn't
deserve it. How did Myles love me anyway, and how was I
going to calm down?

I called Grace from the airport, and she helped me stabilize. I wasn't aware yet of the intensity of my issues, or how to process them. In reality, I was still in survival mode. The gargoyle was gone, but I was still me.

After two days in Durango, it was time to head to Europe. After an easy spin on arrival, I set out to ride the course two days before the race. The course was technical, but everything was ride-able. The reality didn't matter; it was what my mind saw that seemed real to me. Everything was terrifying. My tires were slipping all over the place, I put my foot down on almost every root, and the big rock drop-off looked especially nasty. I got off my bike and just stared at the drop-off. To me, it looked as evil as the gargoyle had felt.

I walked around the drop-off and crashed in the next difficult section. I realized that I'd better get off the course or I was going to really hurt myself. I watched my competitors fly by and just stood there, dazed. I exited the course as quickly as I could and found a field to lie down in. I tried to ground myself, and asked for help from the forest. I couldn't believe how useless I'd felt out there. I talked to a few trees and calmed my spinning mind. I would try again tomorrow.

I couldn't fall asleep. The panic was in full gear. Now I had more fuel to add to the fire. I couldn't even ride my bike. I was going to suck out there. Really suck. I sent Grace a panicked e-mail, asking her to send any help she could. This was bad, really bad. She told me later that she got the e-mail right away; and sent healing, soothing energy my way. At the time, I just trusted that she had, as I gradually calmed down and fell asleep.

The next morning was a brand-new day. I rode everything flawlessly, and my legs felt great. The one thing I avoided was the big rock drop-off. I took the easier but longer route around the obstacle. I knew the drop-off was easy, and almost everyone was riding it, but it still scared me. I knew that the day before, I couldn't ride anything, so I tried to tell myself that the easy way was okay. Fear was fear, and there was only so much I could conquer at a time. Of course, I found a way to beat myself up about not wanting to ride it. I spent most of the day battling the nasty voice that told me I was lame.

The next morning was foggy and cool. The drop was still on my mind, but I hadn't tried it, and race day is not the time to try something new. I told myself I could win anyway. By the end of the first lap, I was leading the race. The spectators booed me every time I went around the drop. It really pissed me off. I felt like screaming, "You have no idea what goes on inside this body! I'm leading the race, so have a little respect!"

Irina Kalienteva from Russia and I were out in front. I led most of the race. She would slip in front of me in the drop section, but I would literally be right on her wheel. I was super strong on the climbs, and I knew I could win this. On the last lap, she attacked me on the climb where I thought I was going to attack her. She got me. I finished 11 seconds behind. I'm sure many people thought I got second because I didn't ride the drop. But I'll tell you why I got second. It was because I wasted energy beating myself up about not riding the drop. I got second because I wasted energy being angry at the crowd. I got second because at the end, I felt I didn't deserve to win if I didn't ride the drop. All of that negative energy and all of that fear drained what I needed in my legs to attack the last climb the way I wanted to. I was second because I didn't believe I was the best.

I was happy, of course, but mostly still angry at myself. What was wrong with me? I was one of the best technical riders in the world, and this weekend it all seemed to leave me. I felt like a beginner. What I know now is that the fear that was coming up in every cell of my body was distorting my entire perspective. It wasn't just about racing—it was my whole life. Everything was about surviving. The racing felt as if my life depended on it. My adrenals were constantly taxed, and I couldn't come down from the high. I felt like I was on constant speed. My metabolism was in overdrive, and my blood sugar was constantly in flux. Being away from home made me anxious about my relationship with Myles, and I was worried about his legal troubles. I had only signed a one-year contract, so I was also worried about money. Everything was on the line again.

I had a difficult week in Belgium. I knew I could win, but I was falling apart. As usual, I kept it together in front of everyone else. No one could believe I had the number 2 plate for the weekend. Number 2 didn't look that impressive to me. I could have had number 1. Maybe that would be good enough for me. Maybe that would calm these survival fears down. I wrote this poem sometime during the week:

> A crystal in my pocket
> My heart on my sleeve
> All the sorrow
> I do reprieve
>
> Free from pain
> And free from tears
> My wheels as wings
> All these years
>
> To inspire
> To be the best
> Long ago
> I was not finished yet
>
> To live a moment
> Time stands still
> The earth my mother
> Cures every ill
>
> I am the win
> I am the sun
> Just begin
> I've already won.

Race day was rainy, and I felt great. I easily made it into the top three by the end of Lap 1.The hills seemed effortless, and the downhills were fun. I was fearless. I had anticipated a battle with Irina, but she was off the pace. Marga Fullana from Spain was with me at the front, and

Eva Lechner from Italy and Lizzy Osl from Austria were
closing the gap. I didn't force the pace. I didn't want to
blow up trying to keep them away from me. We formed a
group of four, and then I launched my attack. I found
myself at the bottom of the downhill with a ten-second gap.
I felt slightly tired, and with a lap and a half to go, I didn't
want the stress of staying out in front.

Eva Lechner rejoined me, and we spent the last lap in a
back-and-forth battle. I was much better on the downhills,
and I tried to get around her on a pivotal one. She put her
elbow out to block me, and I was forced to retreat. We went
into the climb neck and neck. We ran into some lapped
riders, and she squeezed through while I got stuck behind
them. She won by five seconds, but with my two second-
place finishes, I was the World Cup leader.

I was thrilled to be leading the World Cup, but my
feather-weight jersey soon felt like it was full of lead. I
returned home thinking I would be all smiles and joy, but
the waterworks took center stage. There were many
interview requests from all over the world. Mostly they
wanted to talk about the fact that I was the first person to
lead the World Cup riding 29-inch wheels. Most of the
racers used 26-inch wheels, and there were advantages
and disadvantages to each. It seemed to matter little that
my legs and spirit were actually my engine; it all came
down to the wheels. This deflated me, even though I didn't
know it at the time.

A reporter for USA Today wrote a story about me
leading the World Cup without even contacting me.
Basically it said, "When Willow got on her 29-inch wheels,
she turned into Superwoman."

I let it be. People don't usually respond well when you
say, "Actually, I've finally been dealing with my traumatic
past, and I had a gargoyle attached to my collarbone just a
few months ago."

I fell into the old trap of "more is better." I was
exhausted from my spring campaign, but I refused to
admit it to myself, my coach, or my boyfriend. I just kept
pushing. I wanted to keep the leader's jersey, and I wanted
to win a race. I cried because I was tired, and I cried
because I didn't know how to help myself. I only had Grace

on the phone, and sometimes what you need are healing hands on you. I wasn't ready for that in my life yet; I had some of my own work to do.

I arrived in Germany exhausted yet determined. People treat you differently when you have the number 1 plate. In fact, I found it rather annoying. I knew that the minute I wasn't number 1, the attention would fade away, and I would have to resume the task of telling myself that I was great no matter what. That is no easy task when you actually don't believe that.

My race was lackluster. I finished 13th. I had no legs, I had no spark, I had nothing left to give. I had spent so much energy pushing, doing, and striving that I'd shut down my receiving side. I hadn't allowed myself to enjoy being the World Cup leader. I had turned it into a burden, something I had to defend—not something I could enjoy in the moment.

Our feminine side is our allowing and receiving side. Our masculine side is our doing side. I was as feminine as a rock; I was unable to receive, allow, or enjoy. I was deserving of nothing unless I worked hard, struggled, and sacrificed for it. Looking back, it was years of shutting down my feminine energy that had really begun to take its toll. I felt it in my heart, I felt it in my mind, I felt it in my body. But I didn't know what it was. Only that it was painful, and something was breaking. The chasm between my heart and my mind was growing painfully large with every pedal stroke. The closer I got to the top, the more apparent it was that "winning" wasn't the answer. Of course, consciously I knew that winning wouldn't make me happy. But long ago I'd signed a contract with myself that said, "Winning will make you happy, and winning is your only worth."

I had no awareness of any of this during the course of the season, and that unknowing caused me a lot of pain. You learn when you learn, and when the time is right. This was my year of really beginning to see things, and to question the way I had approached my life for all these years.

I was in emotional agony the night after the World Cup. Why it hurt so bad, I didn't know. Now I know it was because all my life I'd been using racing as a substitute for love. When a race is that important, it really hurts when it all goes wrong. There is no salvation from the mental anguish. It's hard to look in the mirror and offer even the slightest encouraging word. My body had betrayed me yet again. I was no longer number 1. I was now riding with plate number 2.

The next morning, with puffy eyes and a wine headache, I set off to do my photo shoot for *Cyclepassion*, a sexy German calendar. I looked forward to somehow feeling pretty and sexy despite how I felt at the moment. I was in a weird place all morning, but when it came time to shoot, I turned it "on."I can be many things, and one thing I loved to be was celebrated for anything other than being fast on a bike. I thought that this was my feminine side coming out to play, but really, photo shoots are still all about doing. As fun as they are, it's all pretense.

The photos were fabulous, and so was I, but I knew it was really just smoke and mirrors. You take the makeup off and then you fly home. Being a sex symbol is not something I'm averse to, but it's a lot to live up to. When you put yourself out there, you open yourself up to being criticized. Along with the praise for looking sexy, also comes jealousy, judgment and blame. A few years earlier, my mom had sent me an e-mail stating her embarrassment and disapproval of my sexier photos. From that moment on, there was a part of me that always held back. Not for me, but in order to get her approval. It was one more thing that was considered "wrong."

In the end, I believe that every "sexy" photo shoot shut down my feminine side even more. I was locked into trying to be sexy, instead of just allowing myself to be sexy. Now I feel I could do a photo shoot and enjoy it for what it is. And if given the opportunity, I will. Then, however, every photo was a loaded gun. I felt the need to have everyone approve of me, and that's an impossible task. You cannot make the people who think sexy is bad, agree with the people who think sexy is good. I wanted my fans to approve of me as much as I wanted approval from my family. But I was fighting a losing battle. On every level of my being, the world was a stage, and the lights were too bright.

There was a break in the schedule, and I got off my bike. I spent two weeks just being a normal person. It felt great, but it didn't last long. I drank too much in Telluride on the 4th of July, and I turned from laughing and being silly into being mad. Really mad. At everything, but mostly myself.

I told Myles the next day that I had no idea I had so much anger inside me. He said he'd had a feeling that was the case. It startled me to think that all these years I'd thought I was so depressed, I was really hiding massive amounts of rage. That evening I looked for a Bach Flower remedy at the health-food store. The "Willow" drops said they would help me to "forgive past injustices" and move on when I felt "resentful and bitter." I took a dropperful right away.

I resumed training, and right away began to do too much. I didn't know yet that my greatest advantage was actually that I needed to do very little to race fast. I didn't believe it. I believed what most others believed, which is that there's no gain without pain. There's no victory without sacrifice, and a champion must suffer. So I did my duty. I did intervals hooked up to an oxygen mask in the hopes of reaching the top step on the podium. One session would have done the trick. I did many. I struggled through my next two National races, and my legs were heavy. I began to panic about the upcoming World Cup in Switzerland. If my legs didn't start to feel better, I knew I was done for.

***

I arrived in Switzerland jet-lagged, with a neck that wouldn't turn left or right. I called Grace, and she worked on me. I began to relax. I told her the course was terrifying, and I didn't know how to ride the drop section. But she told me not to worry about it, that the worry was draining all my energy.

She was right. The rain came pouring down, so I knew race day was going to be muddy. My legs felt amazing, and I just ran down what I was afraid of. I was third, and still second overall. But I managed to give myself a hard time for the rest of the week about not riding the drops. The World Championships were going to be in Switzerland the next year, so I was going to have to face them again. I was really getting tired of being this terrified. It felt like I was going to war every weekend. And I was. I was going to war with myself and my demons, again and again. It felt like I'd been fighting the same fight my whole life.

The next week in Italy, I drank too much wine and didn't eat enough food. I finished tenth. I was now third overall heading into the finals. I thought for sure I could win the finals. I had won the National race there the year before. I had made dirt angels at the finish. I could do this. I arrived home exhausted as usual, and gave myself time to recover. But the recovery never came. I was a favorite to win the finals and the World Championships, but I couldn't even swing my leg over the bike. I was done.

Friends and family told me to calm down. I looked at them like they were crazy. I hadn't gotten to where I was by being calm. No one had any idea what they were talking about, and their advice was driving me crazy. I felt like telling them, "Yeah, that's easy to say when you ride your bike for fun. This isn't fun. This is work. This is my job, my paycheck, my dignity, my sanity, my future, my past, and my life. Don't tell me to fucking calm down."

I went on a few rides with Myles that were supposed to be hard. I tried to do one interval and just stopped in the middle of it. I wanted to throw my bike off a cliff. I had ten days before the races, and I was a crumbling mess. We continued to ride easy, but even that was torture. We stopped under a tree, and I let myself have a panic attack. Myles tried to calm me down. He told me he'd been here before. When you're expected to win, self-sabotage smells dinner. He told me that whether I believed it or not, I was doing this to myself. But I didn't believe him.

That night, I was crying so hard that Myles was worried I wouldn't be able to breathe. "Breathe, baby, breathe!" he shouted at me.

Between sobs, I managed an "I can't! I go 190 beats per minute or nothing. I don't know how to breathe. I don't know how to relax. I can't, I can't!" I cried myself out.

Myles's father was in town for his birthday. He had a bit of insight into my struggles and left the book *Spontaneous Evolution* by Bruce H. Lipton and Steve Bhaerman on the table for me to read. I opened it up to a fascinating chapter on Dr. Leonard Laskow's methods of healing with love. The gist of it was that what we hate the most about ourselves we need to love. Hate causes separation, and separation causes pain. Oneness is freedom, and oneness exists when nothing is good or bad; it just is. Dr. Laskow had been helping sick patients heal by loving their dis-ease into nothingness.

I was intrigued. There was so much I hated about myself and my body that I didn't know where to begin. I looked up Dr. Laskow on the internet and found that he offered sessions over the phone. I called his office immediately and gave his assistant a brief rundown of my past and where I was right now. I told her that I left in five days for two important races that I was expected to win, and I was having a nervous breakdown. She told me she would pass on my story to the doctor and do everything she could to get me an appointment. I hung up the phone and asked the universe to please make this happen. Please.

Dr. Laskow himself called me a few minutes later. He was very interested in my story and wanted to help me. We set up an appointment, and I breathed a sigh of relief. I thanked him from the bottom of my heart.

My appointment with Dr. Laskow was scheduled the day before I left for the World Cup finals. I lay down on my bedroom floor and soaked up some much-needed new information. We talked about my past, and where I was now. We decided to work on my survival issues from the time I was in the womb. I visualized that I was safe and wanted, and that my life was never in question. As he guided me through healing exercises, I gathered more tools for my toolbox.

I learned how to breathe through my heart and connect to everything with love. I learned how to breathe through the back of my head and connect to the infinity of all that is. Dr. Laskow asked what image came to mind when I thought of peace, love, and happiness. I said a rainbow. He then taught me how to breathe each color of the rainbow in through my chakras. If I had any pain, I could send a rainbow from my heart to the area of frustration, and let it disappear.

Whenever I would see a rainbow now, it would be a reminder to breathe, and to ask myself if I was living from my old robotic consciousness, or my new awareness. My body felt sparkly and diamond-like.

I had to end the session to pick Myles' son up from school, so Dr. Laskow reminded me to drive carefully. As I pulled up into the carpool line, the license plate in front of me was from Hawaii. The instant manifestation of a rainbow from the universe made me smile. I realized right then that the jersey of the World Champion was also a "rainbow jersey." My legs were feeling lighter by the second.

***

At the airport on my way to New York, I walked by a newsstand that had the international cycling publication *Velo News* front and center. On the cover it said: "World's Fastest Lingerie Model." I wondered if that was the story they'd interviewed me for a few weeks ago. It was. In the centerfold was a photo of me in a field with a superimposed rainbow over me. Under me, the rainbow turned into the colors of the World Champion's jersey. The title of the article was "Remaking Willow." I started at it in disbelief. Another rainbow. I inhaled every color and continued on to my departure gate.

I felt fine in New York, but not my best. The good part was I stayed calm. I was third overall going into the finals, and I could be number one if I had a fantastic race. I was in fourth most of the day, but faded to sixth on the last lap. It was good enough for second overall. I was relieved. I hadn't been able to train in a month, and my fitness was better than I had expected. Next week was the World Championships in Mt. St. Anne, Quebec Canada. Next week I wanted to win.

That year was different. I wasn't the underdog, I was a favorite. I used my new "tools" to forget about the month I'd spent trying to train in vain, and focused on seeing rainbows wherever I could. I actually breathed. There's an infamous rock descent on the Mt. St. Anne course, and I knew I needed to ride it right away before it started to scare me. Luckily, the track was dry and I couldn't believe how easy it was to ride. I felt happy. Mostly I felt happy that I wasn't afraid.

I picked Myles up at the airport, and we had a nice dinner in Quebec. He'd never seen me in an international race before, and I was extra motivated to show him that I was amazing. We rode the course the next day, and it was dry and perfect. Again, my confidence was rising. My legs were feeling good. Maybe the demons would leave me alone for once.

The day before the race, we woke up to a drizzle. Rain makes the rocks slippery, and I knew that. I was a bit nervous, but I knew how to ride the track. As soon as I lined up to go into the rocky descent, my front wheel turned back on me, and I was on the ground. I completely freaked out. What the hell did I just do? I couldn't decide whether to get back up to the top and try again or just get off the course. I was so pissed. I told Myles we were going to do it again, but the course marshal blew the whistle at me and yelled, "Course closed!"

I was burning up inside. Shit, I was going to have to go to sleep the night before the World Championships thinking about wet rocks and crashing. Damn it, I should have stayed off the course altogether.

Myles tried to calm me down as we rode on the bike path, but I was practically hysterical. He told me to stop and put my bike down. So I did. He picked up a stick and literally drew a line in the sand. He showed me that I had taken the turn too far to the inside, and that's what caused my wheel to turn back on me. He showed me that by going up higher on the rock, I would make a wider turn and my wheel would have time to straighten out before I hit the rough descent. He also told me that I'd been riding the line perfectly all week, so I should stop obsessing about it. His pep talk helped, and I relaxed a little. I still managed to drink almost an entire bottle of wine that night. The voices were just that loud.

I awoke with banging on my door. The International Cycling Union (UCI) wanted to test my blood. I couldn't freakin' believe it. The UCI collects random blood samples to make sure the athletes are not doping. I knew that very few of my competitors were getting their blood drawn that morning. It wasn't fair. This was time to eat my breakfast and visualize the race. I needed every drop of blood and energy I could get! But I didn't have a choice. You cooperate or you don't race. I didn't say a word to anyone. It was clear I was unhappy. After the test, I was frazzled and dizzy. I was late to eat my breakfast, and it was still raining.

As I was warming up on the trainer, Myles hiked up to check out the rock section. He sat there for a while and felt the vibe of the area. He touched the rocks and walked the line. He came back to tell me that it was good to go. I could ride it, I needed to ride it. He knew that fear drains energy, and he gave me all the reason in the world to ride with confidence. I trusted him and didn't give it another thought. Today, the easier and longer way was not an option.

I went to the starting line still in a daze. This was it. This was the last race of the year. Somehow, someway, I was going to make all this torture worth it. I wouldn't leave anything out on the track. As the gun went off, I found myself comfortably in the lead. I slipped back a few places before the top of the climb, and went into the rocky descent behind less skilled riders. I rocketed down the slabs of wet rock and ran into the back of a rider who was running. I crashed on my butt but got right back up. That wasn't my fault, and I knew it. The rocks were safe, and I was good to go. I picked off riders and finished the first lap in the top three.

I don't remember everything about the race. But this is what I do remember: I wasn't afraid. At all. I was locked into some sort of zone, and I felt protected and primal. I felt like a savage. I wasn't worried about scratching myself or getting a bruise. I wasn't worried about hurting. I was hunting, and I was hunting to kill. My legs felt empty, yet full of light. I could hear the cheers of those who knew me, and I looked at them to acknowledge their presence. I was fully in my body, and it gave me power. This was me, living my life. This was me, appreciating my talent, my opportunities, and this moment. I was free.

Maja Wloszczowska of Poland had a slight advantage over Catharine Pendrel from Canada and myself, and Irina Kalentieva from Russia was just behind us. It was a tight race from start to finish. Nothing was for sure, and there were only three medals at the finish line. Fourth wasn't good enough. And I wanted to win. I saw Maja head into the fast woods section, and I picked up the pace. We were closing down on her, and I was getting splits for confirmation. Just as I went into the woods, Catharine came charging at me from the left side. It was either slow down or run into the tree she was driving me toward. I hit the brakes.

"Catharine!" I yelled, and then I took a breath. I didn't want to waste my energy being mad at her. I would just beat her. We lost time in the woods section—I knew that before I was told. I was on the brakes behind her trying to be patient. I passed as soon as I could. I could still see Maja, but she was farther ahead now. I put my head down to chase.

Catharine and I spent most of the race together. I always took the shorter but more difficult line on the descent, while she opted for the easier route. On the second-to-last lap, I finally got a gap on the descent. I held it to the finish line and headed out for the final lap. I was 30 seconds behind first with a good 15 to 20 seconds on Catharine and Irina. I had the silver in my hands, but I still chased for gold. I was closing. At the top of the climb, I had gained ten seconds. I was getting dizzy from the effort. I breathed deeply and headed into the descent. Maja had been running it every lap, and I knew I could gain more time there. As I headed into the descent, I was suddenly on the ground. I had slipped before I even reached the tricky section, and now my front wheel and foot were stuck in the fencing. I lost my 20 seconds, because right then Irina and Catharine were breathing down my neck.

Someone yelled at Catharine, "It's time!" and she rode the A line for the first time. Irina got off and ran it. I rode the B line. I had no time or composure to clip in and ride safely, as I was in total shock. I had just gone from second place closing in on first . . . to fourth.

All three of us hit the bottom of the last climb together. Defeat was burning in my eyes. Myles was at the bottom of the climb. He looked right at me and screamed, "Do not give up on a medal!"

I swear, I absorbed some of the "red mist" he'd talked about seeing before his downhill races. I stopped feeling sorry for myself and resumed the fight. Irina attacked the climb, and I tried to get around Catharine to follow. There was no place for me to pass. We headed into the last downhill sections, through the feed zone and into a grassy field. A few hundred meters ahead was a large crossover bridge, and then a sweeping left-hand turn into the finish. I didn't think; I just pedaled. I passed Catharine on the left just before the tape narrowed and the crossover bridge appeared. I crested the top in third place and sprinted around the grassy turn to the finish. I had won Bronze again, and again, I was 52 seconds behind.

Once again, relief was my most dominant emotion. What if I'd been fourth? What if I had that disappointment to grapple with all fall and winter? As much as I wanted to win, I was satisfied that I was at least standing on the podium. Myles was proud of me, and we savored the moments between my relief and the inevitable "What if" questions that would arise later. We relished in the respite from the battle, no matter how short lived. I remember going back to the team trailer after the men's race, and Myles was almost asleep in the chair.

"Can we go home now?" he asked. "I'm so exhausted."

I knew just what he meant. This year had taken a toll on both of us. We were done.

When we finally got back to Durango, I remember lying on the floor trying to ground myself. I looked up at Myles and whispered, "I can't do that again. I don't think it was worth it." The universe was listening.

******

9

The End of the Night

I entered the off-season like I always did. I drank to try to calm myself down. My adrenals were always firing, my back hurt, and my mind was restless. The only way I knew how to relax was to pick up the bottle. Of course, I had some tools that helped me, but by the time 5:00 p.m. rolled around, I was so sick of battling my mind that I needed some relief.

Myles's custody date was looming, and the stress was intense. He'd been wrongly accused on numerous counts, and I was longing for the record to be set straight. It's impossible to explain how difficult it is to watch someone struggling in the legal system. There's nothing you can do to help. It's all paperwork and lawyers, judges and family investigators, extensions and delays.

We'd planned on going to Hawaii for a vacation, but the court was set for the day before Thanksgiving. It looked like our break was going to be spent in battle. Dr. Laskow suggested that I practice my transpersonal healing techniques in the courtroom. I could send heart vibes to the judge, the lawyers, the witnesses, and even Myles's ex. The key was to surrender my desired outcome, and trust that the universe would deliver what was necessary for the highest and greatest good of all.

Even though my intended plan was to remove myself from the equation, it was impossible to do so. I was far too close to the scene of the crime. This was the man I loved, this was his life, our life, and I wanted the bleeding and the lies to stop. As soon as the morning session began at 9 a.m., I began to spread heart vibes around the courtroom. As the family investigators took the stand, it became very evident to everyone that Myles and his son were the victims in this case. His ex had committed serious and damaging acts of parental alienation and had been lying to the cops, the lawyers, and the court. I relaxed a little, knowing that no judge could hear all this and not do the right thing.

We took an hour for lunch and went back to court until 5p.m.The judge said that he couldn't reach a verdict that day, and sent us home to wait. My clothes were soaked with sweat, and I was alternately burning up and freezing. Again, the only thing I felt I could do was lie on the floor. So that's what I did. We spent Thanksgiving day with our friends, and woke Friday morning to an e-mail from Myles's lawyer. A decision had been reached: his son was to live with us and spend every other weekend with his mother. Myles had full decision-making powers, and his ex was to be closely monitored to keep her alienation and deceitful behavior in check. One year later, this case had finally come to a close.

Myles and his son wanted to go snowboarding and asked me to join them. I couldn't. I was so wiped out. Not only had I spent all my energy in the courtroom, I'd spent all my energy worrying about the outcome of the case for a year. Add to that, trying to stay on at top of the mountain-bike standings, battling my demons, and adjusting to life as a pretty full-on "stepmom." If there was breathing room in sight, I couldn't see it. I just wanted a vacation from my life.

About a week after the court date, I went to get a massage. As I was heading into the room, I stopped to look at the business cards set up on the table outside. A card I'd glanced at all summer finally grabbed my attention: "Marie Redfeather, Reiki Master/Teacher, Shamanic and Theta Healing." I threw one in my purse. All summer I'd seen that card, but I kept telling myself that I didn't need any help. I had Grace I could call on, and I was obviously riding fast. My life didn't seem to need deep healing work. Finally, I was beginning to admit that I needed help, even if I wasn't sure why.

I called Marie the same day. She returned my call immediately, and I booked an appointment for later in the week. I felt like I'd just committed to something huge. And I had. When you sign yourself up for shamanistic work, you are signing up for work. Shamanistic work involves digging to the bottom, seeing things you'd rather not, and facing fears that seem as large as a tsunami. I didn't know this at the time, but I felt it.

I'm not sure now what Marie and I discussed during our first session, but I do know that I gave her a pretty detailed overview of my life and my current issues. She recommended that we start with a light body healing. What this meant is that she would be tapping into my seven-layer auric body system, and pinpointing where in the "blueprint" of my aura, false beliefs and traumas had trapped themselves in my energy field. She said that it was important for all human beings to realize that we are all energy; and that when we can grasp this concept, energy healings become the only real healings anyone needs.

After our session, Marie suggested that I schedule a soul retrieval. She told me that people with a traumatic childhood have usually lost part of their soul during, and through, the trauma. I was more than willing to reclaim my power. I felt like I'd spent a lifetime trying! We scheduled my soul retrieval for after the Christmas holidays, and she encouraged me to begin an anger-release ceremony. She told me not to be afraid of emotions that might come up— I'd stirred the pot by letting her into my auric energy fields, and sometimes it gets messier before it gets better.

No kidding. That same night I felt anger boiling up in me that I'd never felt before. I'd only begun to acknowledge my anger a few months ago, and now it was overtaking me like some kind of drug. It scared me. I called Marie, and she told me this was a good sign. She suggested I beat a pillow and scream and just let it out. I thanked her and hung up the phone. I took it one step further. I grabbed a knife from the kitchen and shut my door. I stabbed the shit out of my fancy memory-foam pillow. Tears were streaming down my cheeks, and I couldn't believe how good it felt to shred that pillow to bits. I collapsed on my bed and just let the calm wash over me.

Myles had been downstairs in his room with the door shut, terrified of what he was hearing. I told him I was sorry, but that I'd started a healing that I couldn't turn back from, and my job was to let my emotions out. I'd been bottled up so tight for so long that real healing was going to require me to get messy. I had to let myself feel out of control. I had to allow grace to enter my life. I'd been resisting my "stuff" and running on anger and feelings of worthlessness for too long. The old way wasn't going to work anymore, and I didn't want it to. I had no idea what the new way was, but that uncertainty is what I needed to trust the most.

Myles respected me for facing my demons, and he was inspired to do the same. We could do this together .And we did.

My healing trajectory is a bit of a blur from that moment on. It seemed like one thing after another was coming up within me, and I had the strength to face the task head-on. I wasn't scared of my demons and imperfections anymore; I just wanted to get to the bottom of them. It was like peeling an onion, and the layers kept falling off. At times, I would find myself asking, "Now what?"

I held three anger-release ceremonies, each of which lasted three days. The ceremonies were conducted on my own, with clear instructions from Marie. I chose the first person who came to mind, and wrote a letter letting out every bit of anger I had suppressed over the years. I was shocked to see close to ten pages of grievances in front of my eyes.

I then took the letter to a place in the woods and read it out loud. At first I felt no emotion, but by the third day, tears were streaming down my cheeks. At the end of the third day, I burnt the letter and thanked Mother Earth for helping me heal. I repeated this process with two other people. As per shamanic tradition, I can't tell you who those people were, but the important part is that I was no longer letting my anger toward them prevent me from moving forward in life.

Myles began his own work, and I offered encouragement through the emotional rollercoaster that uncovering that kind of anger involves.

My soul retrieval was one of the most intense and liberating experiences I've ever had. I think it took about two hours, but I was in a trance most of the time, so I'm not sure. The ceremony was performed in Marie's sacred healing room, and music was being played on her CD player. The rhythmic beat of drumming allows the mind to fade to the background and one's soul to take over. Messages are clearly channeled to her, and she assists spirit in the healing work.

Before beginning my ceremony, Marie described what would be taking place. She would be journeying backward along a timeline to my original wound. Then she would assist me in reclaiming the part of my spirit that was lost. In the safe space she'd created, she would visit the four sacred chambers of my soul.

The first chamber is the chamber of wounds. Here, Marie would discover the pain of origin. Next, she would stop at the chamber of promises or contracts. In this place, my original soul contract and negotiation would make itself clear. In the chamber of passions, I would discover my joy and life force. In my chamber of treasures, I could reclaim my gifts and possibilities.

During my soul retrieval, my animal medicine, or power, was revealed. The animal spirit guide "Jaguar" was walking by my side, and was in me, around me, and able to guide me through the darkness. I just had to ask. We are all born with animal medicine, but our power can be taken from us during traumatic events. We forget our power and we become sick and weak, vulnerable to psychic attack. Reclaiming one's power is the message of the Jaguar, so Marie recommended studying these big cats as much as I could. I was fascinated and thrilled, as Jaguars had begun to show up on my radar without my knowing why. Jaguar had been there all along, waiting for me to wake up.

My chamber of passions was asking me to draw and paint, and my chamber of treasures was begging me to belly dance. I'd never done either of these things, and as foreign as they were to me, my soul needed them like the desert needs rain.

If someone were to ask me if I was feminine, I would say, "Yes, of course!"I liked to wear heels and look sexy, and I liked beauty products and getting pedicures. But the reality is, that was the extent of my feminine expression. The feminine is about allowing, receiving, and surrendering. I didn't know how to do any of those things.

In fact, allowing, receiving, and surrendering made me feel weak and inadequate. Long ago I'd downloaded a program that said I must fight to survive, and I believed it with all my being. Little by little, the universe was asking me to open up the feminine side of myself. I had the masculine side perfected. I could fight, I could achieve; I could survive, and I could work. The fighter was a master, and my heart was begging for me to let the lover in.

I took my mission seriously. At the time, I didn't know what I was really doing; I just knew it needed to be done. I knew that if I couldn't move my hips in a figure-eight movement, it was something I probably needed to do, so I started dance lessons. It was scary to do this at first, as I was so used to being good at everything. Now, I had to admit that my hips were locked up, and my body really didn't know how to go with the flow. I had to surrender to being taught how to let go, and I had to be willing to be far below perfect. Week after week, I attended class after a session on my bike or skis. Every time I felt my hips move a little more, my heart open a little more, and the ancient goddess within rose to the surface.

I began to paint. I used words as art, and put on canvas what had been suppressed and repressed throughout my entire life. I created a series celebrating sex, and hung it on my bedroom wall. I was beginning to create a sacred space without even realizing it. The days flew by, and 2011 rolled in without much fanfare. Slowly but surely, I began to feel the pressure of another racing season waiting in the wings.

One afternoon I found a small package on my front steps. I opened it to find a small glass bottle that simply said "Restructuring." Enclosed was a note from Myles's mom. She knew I'd been going through a profound transition, and she thought this potion could help. I was intrigued. I took a dropperful and then decided to check out the product's website to see what I'd just put in my mouth.

Before my eyes was yet another sign that I was right on track. Stargazer Li had made my potion, and she also held personal sessions. She was an astrologer who'd made a calendar rooted in the Mayan time cycle called the Tzol'kin.

She created a tool for "keeping time" based on interweaving the 20 Kin (a Mayan word meaning both "sun" and "day") and 13 numbers. Her calendar wasn't linear, but rather, circular. The phases of the moon, eclipses, and planetary movements were all tracked and charted so one could follow the rhythm of the universe.

Each of us was born on a certain day, and with a certain number. With all the talk of 2012 being the "end" of what we know, I was interested in Li's perspective. Given her study of the Mayan way of life, and practicing it herself for many years, she thinks that 2013 will bring about living in the 20/13 rhythm of the Tzol'kin. Humanity has been out of touch for so long that the reconnection with "earth magic" is really what is needed. In other words, 2012 is not the end; it is the beginning. This was just my kind of thing, and I sent her an e-mail to set up an appointment.

Li's questionnaire required me to provide background on my life, as well as what I was doing right now. I called her a few days later, and we talked for two-and-a-half hours. Those were some of the most insightful and transformative moments of my life. I got the hang of the calendar right away; in fact, it spoke to me.

What does Monday and Tuesday mean anyway? I could relate far better to a "wind" day, or a "star" day. I was born on a 7 "night" day. The number 7 stands for attuning to the mystical energies and finding the middle ground at the peak of the pyramid. Night is the deep dreaming darkness where life is imagined into being—a time to go inside one's self; home and hearth, inner richness and abundance: a time for telling stories.

Li explained that so far in my life, I had been very internal. Internal with my trauma, internal with my struggles, internal with my hopes and dreams. As a 7, I would always be striving to be my best, and in fact, the top is where I belonged. It was no accident that I'd decided I wanted to go to the Olympics when I was seven. Life is divinely orchestrated whether we can see that or not.

In the calendar, a life cycle is 52 years. I immediately remembered that I had been 52 seconds behind in the last two World Championships. I also remembered that Myles had grown 52 pot plants. Five plus two equals seven. This was getting exciting. Stargazer Li pointed out that the universe has been showing me signs of significance and synchronicity all along. I couldn't agree more. Within the 52-year life cycle (which you can obviously go around more than once) are 13-year waves. With the arrival of my 33rd birthday a few weeks earlier, I'd just moved out of a 13-year journey in the night. I was beginning a new journey. I was now in the first year of a 13-year journey as a star.

Li told me that with all 13-year transitions come huge shakeups. My life was no different. The intensity of the last year, coupled with my desire to purge, cleanse, and clean up my life, were in direct proportion to the intensity of the transition from living in the dark to living in the stars. My depression, my "victim" mentality, my relationship endings and beginnings, my struggles with racing, and my struggles with myself were all coming to a head. This was the time to change! She told me that all was perfect. Everything I'd been doing instinctually was right on the mark. This was my time to shine. A few of her closing words were: "The darker the night, the brighter the star."

******

10

Crystal Castles, Chrysalis Dreams

I was determined to sparkle. I had new wings to soar on. I went cross-country skiing and back-country snowboarding. And then I got a phone call. Myles was in Phoenix dirt biking with some friends. His message simply said, "Hi, baby, it's me. Call me when you can." I knew something was wrong, I just hoped it wasn't as bad as my imagination was making it out to be.

It turned out he was in the ER with a broken humerus. He didn't know if he needed surgery, but he was going to wait to see his doctor at home. He kept telling me he was sorry, and I kept telling him it was okay. I didn't realize the gravity of things until I actually saw him a few days later. He was really broken. He couldn't work at his construction job for at least two months. He couldn't ride or really do anything for at least two months. His arm just had to hang off his shoulder at a certain position to heal. It was a better option than surgery, but he was in pain, and I was in a panic.

Myles was my training partner and secret weapon. I wasn't sure if I could do it alone. He couldn't work, so the rent and food were my responsibilities. All of a sudden I felt like a single mom. A single mom who was trying to win the World Championships. The winter was cold, gray, and windy. There was a headwind almost every day. Some days were so cold my face would freeze while skate-skiing. But I trudged on.

I called Li again and filled her in. She reassured me that Myles would be okay, and that this time off from work and riding would give him time to reassess, as this year had been very hard on him, too. She encouraged me to explore new ways of training. Without Myles pushing me, I could practice allowing energy in, instead of always expending my own. I could go my own pace and connect with the magic around me. I could do this on my own. And I did. I set the pace, and I let it be easy. I let light in.

107

I looked at my situation as an experiment, but it did little to calm my anxiety. No matter how much I'd hated racing the previous year, I'd always managed to be at the top. I was a little worried about changing so much at once, but that's just the way it was. Li told me that I was in the process of learning "new operating systems," and believe it or not, the old way of operating wouldn't work for me anyway. I didn't quite believe her, but I decided to trust her.

During this time I began to have increasingly intense dreams. My dreams have always been complex, but now they were taking on new meaning. For at least six years I'd had a recurring dream involving tidal waves and panic. The waves would grow higher and higher as I looked over my shoulder trying to run for safety. I could never quite outrun them, but they never crashed down on me.

In 2008, during the collapse of my Olympic dreams, the waves finally crashed down upon me. In this new dream, I was being taught how to dive through waves by a native on an island. I was doing well and having fun. Suddenly the native looked up and said, "How about this wave?" I looked up, but at first I couldn't see it. The wave was so huge that it was touching the sky.

I asked, "How can I possibly dive through that?"

He replied, "The same way you dove through all the others." I took a deep breath and dove through. I kept swimming and swimming with no air. It felt like my chest was going to explode. All of a sudden, the wave turned porous, and I realized I could breathe under water. I relaxed and kept swimming. There was a definitive wall at the back of the wave, and there was a small window with a screen in front of me. I kicked through the screen and crawled out the window. Before my eyes lay the most beautiful paradise I'd ever seen or imagined. After I went through the window, other people starting pouring through as well.

I told Stargazer Li about this dream, and she told me I'd found a portal. Not only that, but I'd faced my fears, had dove in first, and then others had followed my lead.

I escaped the cold and wind for a few days to visit a friend in Laguna Beach. I thought I'd feel great and calm, but the vibes from my years of living there were still activated in my system. I felt jittery, my stomach hurt, and my nervous system was a wreck. I knew I was probably just letting some old stuff come up, so I didn't worry about it too much.

I stopped in to see Grace, and she hardly recognized me. I looked different; I looked like I was there. She told me I was hardly recognizable from the girl she'd met two years ago. I was thrilled to hear that. She encouraged me to practice visualizing more and training less. I was ready for it. Now there were two people who thought it was possible for me to do less and gain more. I still didn't totally believe it. I'd been doing less mileage over the years, but I had certainly increased my effort. I was hanging onto the idea that this was the reason I'd improved my race results. It was surely the reason everyone else wanted to believe.

I returned to Durango and immediately felt frazzled. There was such a huge distinction between my old life and my new life that I felt disoriented. The old fight or flight kicked in. I didn't know if I was up for dealing with Myles and his injury, all the financial pressures, and having a stepson. How could I handle all that and train? I was doubting myself and my life, and I wanted to run. Far and fast.

I was aware of what was going on, and I had to be honest that I was really afraid of commitment. When things got serious and life seemed too real, I wanted out. Myles was hurt and worried. He feared that Laguna had triggered me, and he was right. I called Marie, as there were many things I needed to face.

We talked a lot about what kinds of feelings had come up for me in Laguna—my old body issues, my insecurities, my tendencies to live "on the edge." Marie pointed out that Myles and his son were the best things that had ever happened to me, and my resisting them was really just a way of holding myself away from the things I wanted, but didn't feel I deserved. If I ran away first, no one could run away from me. It was a defensive mechanism, and one that needed to be defused. I was safe, and I needed to feel safe. She suggested that I tell Myles all of my insecurities. It was worth risking embarrassment for me to feel safe being

109

vulnerable. It was me who needed to trust, and only I could do the talking.

I was nervous all day about seeing Myles. I didn't want to have to bring up all the fears I had again. I didn't want to talk about how I was always worried that my body would betray me, and that I felt like I was losing control. I didn't want to talk about how I wanted to run away.I didn't want to talk about how I didn't feel safe. I had talked about all of it before with him, but I was hoping he had somehow forgotten my struggles, and saw me how I wanted to be seen: strong, capable, fierce, and independent. I was hiding from him, and it was killing me.

When he got home, I talked, and he listened. I cried, and he held me. We lay down on the floor, and my body was shaking so bad my teeth were chattering. Myles just said over and over that it was okay, and to just let it out. I felt safer than I ever had before. I was far from perfect; in fact, I was a mess. But he loved me. I hadn't scared him away by being real. Actually, I had strengthened our bond by truly trusting him.

Two days later, Myles proposed. He'd been planning it all along. He sold his motorcycles to buy me a ring. If I hadn't been vulnerable, I would have always doubted if he really knew what he was asking when he proposed. Now I knew—and he knew—that we loved each other no matter what. My demons didn't scare him, and his didn't scare me. Love was bigger than all of that.

They say when you know, you know. I finally got it. It wasn't a question in my mind at all. Here was Myles with his broken arm, and me with my broken heart, and I knew this is what I wanted. I had never felt unconditionally loved by anyone in my life. This man gave it to me every day, no matter what. Even if the rest of my life seemed uncertain, I knew that a love like ours wasn't easy to find. We had wedding plans within a week, and invitations ordered within two. It was easy, and it was fun.

I continued with my training, and new healing modalities found me every step of the way. I met a woman named Donna who had great methods of meditation to share. I was still learning how to love my body, and she knew how to help. I visualized light entering every organ

and cell of my being. She encouraged me to run earth
energy up my body, and sun energy down it while on the
bike. "Less is more," she told me. "You are capable of
grasping this." That was three people telling me the same
thing now, so I was beginning to listen.

Marie suggested we do a 40-day crystal-clear ceremony.
First, you let all the negative beliefs and programming out
of your body and into a crystal with two naturally faceted
ends. Then you cleanse it overnight in salt water. Next, you
write down nine new truths you want to program into your
body. Every day, you hold the crystal and repeat your
affirmations. I was totally into it, so I set out to find my
crystal.

I walked into a store in Durango, and immediately
wanted to buy every crystal in the shop. They were
beautiful, and the air felt clean and wonderful. The owner
(named Crystal!) just stared at me and said, "People listen
to you; you are here for a very important reason."

I looked back at her and said, "Wow, thanks." She
asked what I did for a living, and I told her. She said I
should bring in my bikes for a blessing. She handed me
crystals that Spirit was telling her I needed. I loved it, I
loved her, and I loved that space. I left the store with my
new crystals, floating high, feeling fabulous.

I bought an altar, set it up in my room, and put the
crystals on it. I found a Jaguar sculpture and put him on
the altar as well. Marie gave me some beautiful owl
feathers, and I added that to the mix. I wrote my desires on
paper and put them on the altar. I then stated my
intentions and let them be important.

I trained, I breathed, I listened. The Jaguar was
becoming a part of me now. In my sessions with Marie, I
could actually feel that my back was soft to the touch, like
a Jaguar's coat. When I closed my eyes, I saw his green
eyes. He could eat up fear and transmute pain. As nothing
can be created or destroyed, transmutation is the most
powerful form of healing. I understood that, and I
encouraged it. What we fight against becomes bigger than
we are. When we realize that within us lies the entire
universe, we stop pushing against everything and start
allowing ourselves to feel joy.

For the first time in my life, I was allowing good things to come to me. I didn't question if I deserved Myles. I didn't question if I deserved to be healthy and happy. I didn't question if I deserved to win. I felt a resounding yes throughout my entire being. I was open, I trusted the universe, and I had surrendered to the beauty of my life.

A few weeks before leaving for South Africa, my intuitive massage therapist said she smelled children around me. She said they smelled like sugar cookies. She looked at my palm and said I would have two children, and they would be close together. I thought that was nice. I had wondered if I would ever have children due to the damage and stress I'd inflicted on my body.

I took my bikes in for a blessing, and it was beautiful. I named my bikes River, Feather, and Star. Crystal said I should bow to my bikes before every competition. I had been a warrior; now I was a warrioress.

Myles and I sent out invitations and opened a bottle of champagne. I left for South Africa the next morning.

Six weeks later, I found out I was pregnant. I was a zombie. I was alone. I was confused. I came home. I tried to be okay. But I wasn't. I saw the e-mail from Martin. And then I fell apart.

******

11
Death and Rebirth

From the moment I looked at that e-mail from Martin saying that the sponsors were reviewing their investments and that we needed to talk, my world began to unravel. The survival fears were once again triggered, but this time it wasn't just a fear, it was real. My career was in question, and so were my finances. My body was changing by the day, and I felt control slipping out of my hands. I was exhausted. My "self" no longer seemed to exist. My identity had been wrapped up in bike racing, and without it I felt worthless.

In my mind, I wasn't sexy anymore because I didn't feel sexy. I felt like a dirty old rag. My body was, in fact, trying to survive. I had put it through the ringer in South Africa . . . training, racing, being sick, and of course, getting pregnant. I had cut way back on my calories thinking my stomach bloat would disappear. When I came home, my body was screaming at me to care for it—not to mention my unborn baby.

It was hard to listen. I didn't want to listen. I wanted my old life back, no matter how full of pain it was. This was too much to bear. At first, I had no idea why I felt so dead. I could see the outside reasons, like stress and pregnancy, but I had no idea why I literally felt like I was dying inside. Slowly but surely I slipped further down into despair. For a few days I could drag myself out of bed for a few minutes, but that was about it. My face broke out in a horrible rash, and that was the limit for me. I was shaken up enough to call Marie. She came over to my house that afternoon. I told her what was going on, and how I was so out of it I didn't even think to call her. It took blisters on my face for me to take any action at all. Otherwise I would have just lain there.

Marie explained to me that what I was going through was called a "shamanic death." She reminded me that I had called on big medicine, and that I was capable of moving through this no matter how hard it seemed. She reminded me that I had asked for a complete healing, and this was the direction in which I needed to go. A shamanic death consists of the end of your life as you know it: the loss of a job, an identity, security, and previous beliefs are some of what one can expect. As challenging as this is, it is a total cleansing and purging of what no longer serves one's highest and greatest good. The subconscious cannot stay hidden for long in this scenario, and the inevitable healing crisis is waiting to happen. The more one resists, the tougher it is. So it's better to dive right in.

So that's what I did. We talked about the significance of my face breaking out in a rash. My old "mask" was peeling off, and my real face was trying to show itself. What I thought was "me" for so long was only an illusion. I was not a sexy bike racer; that was only a label. Who I really was, was much deeper than that. Who all of us are is much deeper than something like that. We are source energy in a physical body. We came to this world to experience being human, but we are pure energetic love. We are born in this state, but through years of human conditioning, we come to believe that we must achieve to receive love.

Throughout my life, I had attached self-worth to results, perfection, and approval. I would have done anything to get others' approval, and when they didn't approve of me, my world would crumble. And consequently, I'd never learned to approve of myself. I subconsciously decided that to be worthy of love, I must constantly prove it.

The subconscious believes what you tell it to believe. I never questioned this way of thinking; it was my truth. Every choice, every action, and every breath I took was solidifying this false belief into my being. I was no longer love; in fact, I was convinced I didn't deserve it. The person who treated me the worst in my life was myself. I was my slave driver, and I was the task master. I was never good enough for me, so how could I ever be good enough for someone else? I had created a reality that I couldn't escape. The only escape was a complete destruction of what I thought was real.

This was happening, and it hurt. It hurt to see the life I'd built up around me crumbling down. It hurt to admit that I'd locked myself in a prison of my own creation. All those years that I'd thought, "This isn't worth it, I'd been right." But this was my path to healing. Every step of the way, I had opened myself up just a little more to let the light in. I'd been begging for this, crying for this, desperate for this. I'd always been searching for relief, and now it was my choice. I could struggle, continuing just as I had been, or I could find relief in the death of the old.

At first, I resented the challenges ahead. It was easy for me to feel sorry for myself. I was the only person I knew with a story just like mine, and it was easy to feel like a victim. I had to pull myself out of that quickly and see that I'd been given a gift—the gift of a new life. This was my chance to create a world I wanted to live in, and a world I wanted to see. With death comes rebirth.

First, I admitted how disappointed I was. I wanted to win bike races. It is all I ever really wanted to do. I didn't dream of being happily married with a family. I dreamed of winning. I knew I could come back if I really wanted to, but first, I had to let it go completely. I had to be okay without it. Better yet, I had to be great without it. I had to learn that there were actually things about myself I could love. My usual escape routes were closed off. I wasn't training, racing, traveling, or drinking. I wasn't doing photo shoots and being told I was sexy. I wasn't being called for interviews. I was left on my own, and I had to look in the mirror and find something to like. I'd been running away from myself my whole life, and now it was back to square one.

I had to love and comfort the little girl I used to be. I had to let her be sad, angry, and scared. I had to love the teenage me, the one who was chubby and insecure. I had to love the self-destructive me who threatened to kill herself. I had to love everything that I wished wasn't real. I had to look at those paper doll "Willows" and give them life. I had to accept and nurture them. I had held them apart from me, and that distance had caused enormous pain. We all had to unite as one.

With separation there is pain; with unity there is peace. It was time to love everything I hated about myself. It was time to appreciate the lessons I'd been gifted to learn. It was time to love me for being nothing other than alive. There was nothing to fight for this time; it was about surrendering.

I called Dr. Laskow and related my struggles. He said simply, "You used racing as a substitute for love." It's amazing that such a simple and truthful observation took more than 20 years to uncover. I was bound to my truth that I was unworthy, and only through my suffering would I finally break the chains and be free.

Rumi, one of my favorite poets, said: "When my pain became the cause of my cure, my contempt changed into reverence and my doubt into certainty. I see that I've been the veil on my path. Now my body has become my heart, my heart has become my soul, and my spirit, the eternal spirit."

I had always thought I hated bike racing, but now I needed to love it. I needed to love it for the challenges it brought me, so my wounds could come to the surface. I needed to love it for the people it brought into my life, and the strength it had brought out in me. I needed to love it for beating me down so I could get back up. I needed to love it for being taken away from me so I could see what I needed to see. I needed to free bike racing from the baggage of my soul, and let it fly away. It could come back to me someday, but for now, it had served its purpose.

Dr. Laskow encouraged me to write. He told me I had a story I needed to share. Most of us have substitutes for love, even if we don't realize it. Success, fame, money, things, the big house, the fancy car, the promotion, and the "perfect" relationship are all used to fill a void. There's nothing wrong with wanting any of these things, but most of us aren't aware enough about why we want them. When pursued from a place of lack, they end up owning us. In the case of bike racing, if you come from a place of love, you can play the game. If not, the game will play you.

So I began to write. I knew I wanted to tell much more than my life story, but I knew I would need to share those details first. I called on my personal spirit guides to help me in my mission. I wanted to write a truth for the highest and greatest good of all.

I began to seek out ways to nurture my body and my baby. I learned more about Jin Shin Jyutsu and began to practice it on my own. Jin Shin is the art of harmonizing life energy with gentle touch. There are 26 energetic locks on our bodies, and Jin Shin provides a map of the pressure points one can touch to release blocked energies.

I began acupuncture again and signed up for ten SOMA massage sessions. SOMA massage is deep bodywork combined with emotional-release techniques. As the body and mind unwind, trapped emotions and trauma are released from the muscles and the psyche.

I learned relaxing yoga postures that I could hold for 15 minutes or more. Step by step, I learned how to be in my body and love the changes that were occurring every day. I let myself be in awe of the life growing inside of me. Myles thanked me every day for "giving us a baby."

I returned to the crystal shop for a reading. It had been a long time. Crystal asked me how the race in South Africa went, and I laughed and told her I was pregnant. She told me she could not "see" me in the race, but didn't know why. I went to the back of the store with her and just let her channel Spirit. The first thing she said was, "They are telling me there is going to be a book. In fact, there are three books, but one you must write now and get it out with godspeed."

My face broke out into the biggest smile, and I just continued to let her talk. She told me many things I needed to put in this book, and she encouraged me to be raw and honest. She told me to include my disappointment and not hold back on the drama. I listened, and I wrote some more.

***

With every end, there is a new beginning. This is the beauty of being alive. When we stop growing, changing, and evolving, this is death. Like a butterfly, we grow new wings with every season. Looking back on my life, every challenge has presented a huge opportunity for growth.

Without fear blocking my view, all situations can be looked at with love.

And love for the self extends to everyone. When we love ourselves unconditionally, we learn to love others unconditionally as well. When love is the center of our beings, we can race and have fun. Our achievements will not define us; they will only inspire us. The word "inspire" means "in spirit." To be inspired is to be who we really are.

Through the crisis of the unknown, I found myself. I redirected my focus into writing and being healthy. I was always interested in health, but more because I wanted to be beautiful, fast, and skinny. Now I needed to approach health from a different perspective. It wasn't about a certain weight anymore; it was about nourishment. I had never nurtured myself, and now I had a baby to nurture, too. I had to sit in the car and meditate before stepping on the scales at my midwife's office. This was something I couldn't control anymore. I was going to gain weight; my baby needed me to. I knew this was a huge trigger for me, and I told myself how brave I was for facing this challenge.

I took a private Angelic Reiki class from Marie, and she attuned me to the sacred symbols and the Seven Sisters of Angelic Reiki Healing. I could now practice Reiki on myself, my baby and Myles. My baby inside me loves it when I do Reiki. There is movement and kicks and energy flowing all around my belly. It has been such a joy for me to see how easily we can connect.

I began to Reiki my food so it would be blessed, and I could be relaxed about eating. I wrote goals down on paper, gave them some Reiki, and put them on my altar to manifest.

After a few months had gone by, Martin wanted to speak to me on the phone. I didn't know what his stance was, but I knew I would do my part to create what I wanted. I wrote down my desires on a piece of paper. I wanted my full salary and my two-year contract, and I wanted his full emotional support during this time in my life.

I did some Reiki on my wishes and put a crystal on top. The phone rang, and I answered it. We had a great talk, and he was fully supportive. He'd had to stick up for me when other sponsors wanted him to bail. He has a wonderful heart. He asked me if I felt like I deserved my full salary for the year, and I told him yes. I was blessed to channel many wonderful reasons why I was worth it, and he agreed with me.

I believe that without the time and uncertainty to test me, I would never have believed that I was worth anything at all. What looked like a curse had really been a blessing. I now really believed in me. Not Willow the bike racer, but just me.

I have not reached a point of eternal bliss; rather, I have surrendered to what life is serving me, knowing I can meet it. It is not about arriving at a certain place on the podium, a certain weight, a certain degree of financial stability, or a certain level of fame and glory. It is about knowing that I am worthy of unconditional love—with or without these things.

Most of all, I deserved unconditional love from myself. We all do. We are worthy just because we are alive. We chose this realm to experience Spirit manifested in our physical bodies. It is our birthright to receive and give pleasure, to open our hearts to love, and to see the beauty in every challenge in front of us. We asked to come here, and our wish was granted. Now it is up to us to make this world a place we want to be.

There are many theories and speculations on what 2013 will bring. Change is needed, but the end of the world is not needed for that to happen. If we can change, the earth will change with us. I agree with Stargazer Li that the change we need to embody is an energetic change. We need to be open to living and breathing the energy of the universe. Mother Earth is asking for our attention, and we need to give it to her.

We have become so far removed from what is good for us. Technology has replaced human relationships, and success is measured in money and power rather than the amount of love we have in our lives. Our ideas of success have become distorted, and our souls are suffering because of it. What we need is a wake-up call. I know many people have been feeling the intensity of the times. We are being shaken to the core so that what no longer serves us can be left by the wayside. We now have the opportunity to move forward with open eyes and hearts, and to embrace what the cosmos is offering us. We are pure energetic love, and it is time to remember who we really are.

My friend Crystal has described the times we are living in as "mass destruction due to the greed of the corporate penis."And she is right. You do not have to be a man to engage in this type of behavior. What is overwhelmingly evident is that most of us have forgotten the power of our feminine goddess, and have handed over all our magic and power to doing, achieving, and conquering. We have shut down our allowing side to such extremes that Spirit is finding a hard time accessing our hearts at all. We have been in lock-down mode: blinders on, charging forward to claim our prize. All the while, our real prize has been withering away inside of us.

Our feminine side has not been nurtured. All of us, men and women, need to embrace our feminine side. The merging of our masculine "doing" energy with our feminine "allowing" energy creates a unity that we have all been searching for. When we are masters of both doing and allowing, we will be all that is.

Inside ourselves is an entire universe. We can be everything and nothing, all in a glorious surrender to who we really are. This message is beautifully conveyed in a quote by Nisargadatta Maharaj: "When I see that I am nothing, that is wisdom. When I see I am everything, that is love. And between these two, my life flows."

When unity is allowed within ourselves, that unity is reflected in the world. Those parts of ourselves that we judge and condemn, feel embarrassed about or wish would disappear need to be accepted with love. When we are free from judging ourselves, we are free from being separate from ourselves. The pain we feel is the separation from who we really are. There is no perfect platform we must arrive at. There is no vengeful God who will strike us down when we stumble. The only judge in our lives is really ourselves. We must take responsibility and be our own witness. We must care about how we feel so much that we guide our words, thoughts, and behaviors by the vibration they activate within us.

Life is not easy. I believe in the Law of Attraction, but I also believe that our soul path trumps all of that. It's important to get in a good-feeling place, and to let our desires be known. If, however, life has other plans for you, you must trust the infinite wisdom of the universe. There is a beautiful synchronicity in the ups and downs of life. Spirit will always orchestrate and choreograph how to make your dreams true. Our job is to do our part, and allow the rest to unfold. We need to trust. We have all worked so hard, and attempted to attain so much, that we've forgotten that the universe wants to help us. We've shut down our connection to the cosmos in such an extreme way that we've developed enormous fear and anxiety in the struggle to survive.

We have falsely believed that we have to do this alone. But we are not alone. There is so much magic, grace, and beauty waiting for us to tap into, and we just need to begin to let it in. Bit by bit we can unravel the subconscious beliefs we have been operating on for so long. In fact, we may find that our old ways of approaching life just aren't working anymore. Well, they're not meant to. We're being asked to do away with our old operating systems and to surrender and trust that a new and better way will be shown to us. It is this surrendering and trusting that embodies the feminine nature we so desperately need to embrace.

***

I was so far away from trust of any kind that the universe decided to surprise me with the ultimate feminine gift. An unplanned pregnancy is the height of allowing. Allowing new life to grow inside you is an act of complete surrender.

And I've noticed that the surrendering doesn't stop. Every day I must surrender more, trust more, feel more, and love more. That is what is being asked of me. I think that is what is being asked of all of us. If we can trust that we are divine, that we are provided for, that we are loved, we can all lay down our swords and surrender to the life we are really meant to have.

This doesn't mean that we do not have goals, dreams, or ambitions. All of these things are glorious. It just means that we have our dreams, we do our part, and then we surrender to the outcome. We don't always know what's best for us, and it's time that we let go of a need to know.

Life is ever-unfolding and always evolving. Opening up to the magic that wants to come in will free us from thinking we have to control it all. We are all divine beings of light; we are protected and cared for, and we deserve to feel good.

Unpredictable blessings are around every corner, but so often, blessings come disguised as a curse. I cursed my life and my challenges over and over again. I cursed bike racing for causing me emotional and physical pain. I was very much the stone in my own path. Every aspect of my life has led to this moment right now. I now realize how blessed I am. Every difficulty has allowed me to shed another layer of discontent. Every challenge has called for me to seek a new way of navigating through it. My life has made me who I am, and I am finally proud to be me.

I am not proud because I'm perfect. I'm proud because in spite of all my imperfections, I can treat myself with love. This love has radiated far beyond me, and more and more love is flowing my way every day.

In the end, medals are just dust collectors. I've finally learned to love, and love is the investment of a lifetime. Love becomes greater with time . . . and more sparkly with appreciation.

Love begets love, and infinite love is all there really is.

******

12
A New Athlete for a New World

With the abundance of new energy coming into the planet, I am learning to train, race, live, and breathe in a new way. As I mentioned before, eventually the old way of pushing fails to deliver the same results.

In the spring of 2011 I woke up in a funk. Myles was home, and we were planning on going for a ride. My mantra of the morning was: "I hate bike riding. I hate it." It was windy and nasty out, and I was sick of pushing myself when I felt like I'd rather not. This was my day to finally learn a lesson, and a big lesson it was.

Myles had just healed from his broken humerus, and he had, maybe, ten rides in him. I'd been training for months. I thought that I'd take my irritation and anger out on him in the bike ride. Up till this point in my life, I'd been able to use my anger as diesel fuel. But not anymore. I felt like shit. I could barely hang on. I kept spewing all sorts of negativity on the bike ride, and Myles was doing his best not to laugh at me. All the while, he was appreciating being on his bike and just going faster and faster. I tried to attack him on the last climb of the day but got nowhere. I looked back at him and yelled, "This is so annoying! I've been training all winter, and you are kicking my ass. I hate this!"

Needless to say, at home I turned on the drama. Blah blah blah. I looked over at Myles, and he was staring at the floor, laughing. I started laughing, too. It really was ridiculous, and so very obvious why I'd reacted the way I did. My body was full of negative energy and low vibrations, yet I expected it to feel light, lovely, and free.

The beauty of these new times is that we are accountable and responsible for how we feel. Now, more than ever, the thoughts we think and the words we say will be immediately reflected in our bodies and in our lives.

In the past, my pain and anger were able to be channeled into training and racing. I'm glad that worked

123

for a while, because I needed a way to transmute this energy. I'm also glad to know that it will no longer work. I am now acutely aware of my feelings. Sometimes the negativity will start out as a small, nagging seed of despair: "I'm tired today . . . I don't really want to do those intervals . . . I'd rather just take a bath."

The key to success is to simply listen. Our bodies are trying to shed old layers of cells, along with old layers of false programming, so we can fly free. It's time to be one with our bodies instead of fighting its messages all the time. Our bodies know that less is more, so it's time for our minds to catch up.

The important concept to grasp is that everything is changing. Desperately clinging onto the past will only cause us more pain. It's comfortable to have a routine, a way of training and a way of thinking. But we must risk being uncomfortable in order to grow. This is another test of faith, but one that we will be rewarded for tenfold.

We all have an internal guidance system—we've just turned it off and looked outside of ourselves for answers and approval. We ask others what they're doing and how light their bike is. We trust coaches to guide us even though they're not in our bodies. We've been looking to the outside world for answers, but now it's time to go within.

The first thing I would advise others to ask themselves when it comes to doing anything in their lives is: "Why do I want to do this?" I think many people would be surprised to find that they don't really know. I certainly didn't know for 20 years what was really driving me. If we don't know what we're driven by, it owns us.

My advice to any athlete (or even any non-athlete) is to really take the time find the answer to this question. When we know, then we can better understand ourselves, and we can better understand how we will respond to certain types of training situations and mental imagery.

Most athletes do too much. I don't think I would be an athlete if I had a tendency to sit on the couch and munch on Fritos. In the words of NIKE founder Bill Bowerman, "No one can coach desire." I've found that desire is the key to knowing how to train, what to eat, when to rest, and how to enjoy my life. Sometimes we shut down our desire mechanism because we think the mind is smarter than our instincts. It isn't. When I'm in touch with my desire, I find a way of training that inspires me.

When desire is running through my veins, I love training. I love intervals and hill climbs, sprints and race-pace rides. When I want to do something, the energy is available to me. When I hem and haw and feel tired but don't admit it, I feel the energy leaving my body before I've even begun. Paying attention to this takes a massive amount of deprogramming and practice. I believed I had to always push myself, never skip a workout, and if I "checked off" my training for the week, I was good to go. This isn't true. It's far better to have three quality workouts a week that are energizing, than six that are depleting. I've realized that with every ride or workout, I'm also training the vibrational energy within me.

If I have six bad workouts, my body will start to feel bad just looking at the bike. It's a natural response to something that doesn't feel good. I'm not saying I never push the limit. What I'm saying is that I let myself feel excited about attempting to push my limit, or I don't do it at all.

The good news is the universe is supporting us. "New" energy is readily available to tap into. We will find that when we listen to our bodies and pay attention to the rhythms of the universe, we can do less and gain more. We can ask ourselves, "What do I love about a good race?" I guarantee that how we felt will be near the top of the list. The trick is to get to that feeling place first, and then perform the action. Allowing well-being to flow through us diminishes the physical effort required.

In the midst of the ups and downs in my life and career, these are the secrets I have discovered. Truth be told, no one really knows what I need. That's for me to discover. When people say, "You need this bike or that bike, it needs to weigh this much, only the lightest people are good climbers, and you better put in the hours," they're coming from a place of fear. They're afraid that if they don't follow the "formula," they won't find success. But what is success, anyway, to me? Isn't success loving what I do and how I feel and finding strength in my individuality?

Before I led the World Cup on a 29er (a bike with 29-inch wheels), many people believed that these bikes weren't meant for top-level competitions. As soon as I was at the top, people starting thinking it was all about the bike. I will tell you right now, all that matters is what I believe. I like to say, "It's not what you choose, but the energy behind your choice that matters most." In other words, if I believe in my bike, my training, and my abilities, I have mastered the secret to manifesting my greatness. If I look around constantly at what others are doing and how they're doing it, I'm giving away my power. Everything I need is already inside me. I have to believe that I'm the best athlete in the world, and then let myself fly. Even if I'm not the very best on a particular day, I can always be my very best me. Nurturing myself with words and actions provides me with more joy than any trophy or medal.

There are plenty of ways to tap into the universal life force. I love to connect with the earth when I'm at a race. I will lie down in the field by the course, or stand with my back to a tree and ask to feel its power. I visualize the whole area chanting my name and sending me energy whenever I ask for it.

We are the earth's acupuncture needles. I run energy from the cosmos through the top of my head, and grounding earth energy up through my feet. I enclose myself in a colorful bubble, and run this energy through myself at every moment. I name my bikes and bow to them before I ride them. I am a warrioress on the start line, and I let my imagination run wild. I play with it and make it fun. It's not the most important thing in life. The truth is, bike racing and all athletics is something we made up. It's not necessarily important in and of itself. It's what we bring to it that matters.

I call on Jaguar to help me transmute any fear into power, and I ask my nine other animal totems for assistance when I can. Elk is helpful when needing endurance, and Owl is useful for wisdom and foresight. We can explore our animal totems or animal medicine with a shaman, or we can let the universe show us what we need to see. Long before I knew of my nine animal totems, Owl

126

showed himself to me. If we're asking to be connected to the cosmos, we will be.

I use Stargazer Li's calendar to tap into the energy of each day. As I go through the cycles of 20 kin and 13 numbers, I begin to recognize them when they show up the next time. I have learned which days bring more energy for me, and which days ask me to relax. I know which days would be better for massage, and which days I should just go find a swimming hole. The Mayans tapped into this energy long ago, and everyone wanted to know their secrets. Their secret is that they asked, and then they listened.

To be a master in any art form, our actions must be inspired simply by our love for how it makes us feel in the moment. Detachment from all outcomes brings true freedom. This is easier said than done, though. In my case, I believe that without racing being "taken away" from me for a time, I would never have been able to get where I wanted to go.

In a way, we need to be able to give up everything in order to gain everything. Ultimately, we need to find the joy of just "being" ourselves, and then the things we "do" can be just that . . . things we do as joyful human beings.

It's also important to realize that we have a choice. We don't have to compete or train. We really don't. It may seem like we do if we've been at it for years, but that's an illusion. If we feel trapped by what we do and who we are, it's a prison only we have the key to. Freedom of choice is always available to us. When we gain enough perspective to see that we're choosing to train and compete, we can free ourselves from the obligation of it all.

I've found that choice changes everything. I didn't know if I wanted to race again with a newborn baby, but time has allowed my desire to be reborn. I now know that I don't have to race, I simply want to. I want the wind in my hair, and I want a chance to be on the start line having shed all the baggage I carried with me for so long. I don't know the outcome, and I don't need to. I've discovered that without bike racing, I'm free, so now I can race and have it simply be that. A race. Not my life, my self-worth, or my future, but simply a ride on a bike. That bike ride provides

127

limitless opportunities to explore the energy of the universe and the unlimited potential of the cosmos. And that is what I love.

I've had plenty of issues with food in the past, but I've now learned to love it. Love is the key, as always. I choose organic high-vibe food whenever I can. I make sure to bless my food and thank it for its energy. When I eat meat, I spend extra time blessing it so that the animal's energy doesn't clash with mine. Again, how I feel is everything. Some people will say, "You need this or that to be healthy." If it hurts my stomach or makes me feel lethargic, I pay attention. My body tells me what it needs.

The whole trick is not separating the mind/body from the soul. Our bodies are not the enemy, and they will not betray us. I can't tell you how many times I've heard a fellow racer "hoping" that their legs feel good tomorrow. Why are we so worried that they won't? Our legs aren't separate from us, they are us. Simple reprogramming techniques can help take the anxiety out of racing. I tell myself that my legs always feel great and that my body is my friend. I repeat it over and over until I feel the truth of that statement! I can do this with any negative thought. It takes effort, but as I said, it's a different kind of effort. I don't let my body be lazy, so I try not to let my mind be lazy either.

We need to love ourselves. When we have a hard race, we must quickly find something to be joyful about. We need to appreciate what our bodies are capable of doing for us, and nourish them and lavish love upon them. We should treat ourselves like gods and goddesses, and know that we have the potential for miracles and magic within our very beings. We must respect the life within in us and be thankful for the opportunity to express our passion through sport.

We are lucky to be alive—these are very exciting times!

******

13

Afterword: Freedom

This is the 13th chapter. Some people think 13 is an unlucky number. I think the number 13 is beautiful. It is the number of the goddess. In Jin Shin Jyutsu, the number 13 represents fertility and the ability to love your enemies. On the Tzol'kin calendar, 13 represents the matured self lifting off into flight, reclaiming freedom, transcending, moving beyond boundaries and back into all that is.

When the inspiration for this book came to me, I outlined13 chapters in less than five minutes. I woke up at about three in the morning with jetlag from my trip home from South Africa. As soon as I'd put together the outline, I fell asleep immediately. I believe in destiny, and I believe in purpose. I look for the magic in everything. To me, it is magical that this book is about my journey toward freedom, and the last chapter of this book represents that as well. It makes me smile.

Throughout the writing of this book, I've been giving birth to an aspect of myself that has been buried deep within. The subconscious beliefs that have driven me were meant to become conscious, and I was finally ready to see. It is an amazing feeling to realize that what you fear the most can be dissolved with love and compassion for the self.

A woman's true power comes from love and nurturing. We must encourage all women to love themselves so that they can teach their children how to love themselves, too. Mother Earth needs the return of the goddess. Men and women can learn to nurture their goddess nature, for when we are god and goddess, we are all that is. Then there is no separation within ourselves, and there is no separation between individuals. The tears we have all cried fill one big ocean, and we are all riding the waves together.

The Rumi quote at the beginning of this book ("The wound is the place where the light enters you") has inspired me to tell the truth about my wounds. Without my wounds, I would never have sought a way to heal the pain. Without my wounds, the desire for wholeness would not have made itself known. Without my wounds, I would never have been able to share this story . . . and hopefully inspire others.

Who we are begins in the womb, and I am blessed to nurture new life with grace and wisdom. I am now birthing a book, a baby, and a new me.

I've been given an opportunity to experience a love that transcends bike racing. I've been given the opportunity to love unconditionally and to allow others to love me unconditionally as well. I have the opportunity to be free from the chains I've wrapped around my neck, and I am grateful. I believe we all come to this planet with a script of our choosing. There is no challenge put it front of us that was not perfectly designed for our request to heal and be free. If we can remember that life is about evolution, we can move forward with confidence and faith, even in the darkest hour.

The end of one cycle is always the beginning of another. With open hearts, we can meet the moment, for in this moment is life itself. We can choose to live in the magic of our existence and be in awe of the divine. The goddess within is asking us to allow the beauty of our lives to unfold. She is asking us to trust, to feel, to love, and to heal.

What used to seem like my entire life is now but a piece of my story. Most of what I face now is the unknown. A marriage, a baby, a stepson, and a comeback to the sport of bike racing are all mysteries to me. I am choosing to be thankful for those mysteries and to trust that the universe in its infinite wisdom knows exactly what I need.

Sometimes we ask the universe for what we need, and then when we get it, we start to doubt. In these moments, I think we should leap right off the edge. We will be shown how to face what's next—every time.

I will race next year, and I will race free. No matter the outcome, my bike has been an integral part of my life and my healing. My wheels have given me wings.

***

I hope this book has encouraged you to find the passion in your heart, as well as the courage to love and nurture yourself. The power is within you, and is all around you. You are always supported, and you are loved. May your next ride be filled with awe and wonder, and may you find the magic that has always been inside of you.

In this lifetime and beyond, I wish you love and happiness.

The beginning . . .

Willow

3228832R00075

Printed in Great Britain
by Amazon.co.uk, Ltd.,
Marston Gate.